A Baker's Dozen
By Richard Tydeman

Ali's Barbara
Spring Song Singers
Sea Side Trippers
Snow White Special
Albert Laddin
Ask a Silly Question
Fiesta Fandango
Forty Winks Beauty
Iron-Hot Strikers
Piccalilli Circus
Red Hot Cinders
Way Out West
What-Ho Within!

WWW.SAMUELFRENCH.CO.UK

Ali's Barbara copyright © 1957 by Richard Tydeman, Spring Song Singers copyright © 1955 by Richard Tydeman, Sea Side Trippers copyright © 1957 by Richard Tydeman, Snow White Special copyright © 1955 by Richard Tydeman, Albert Laddin copyright © 1959 by Richard Tydeman, Ask a Silly Question © 1964 by Richard Tydeman, Fiesta Fandango © 1959 by Richard Tydeman, Forty Winks Beauty copyright © 1956 by Richard Tydeman, Iron-Hot Strikers © 1961 Reprinted 1970 by Richard Tydeman, Piccalilli Circus copyright © 1964 by Richard Tydeman, Red Hot Cinders copyright © 1955 by Richard Tydeman, Way Out West copyright © 1957 by Richard Tydeman, What-Ho Within! copyright © 1958 by Richard Tydeman
All Rights Reserved

ALI'S BARBARA, SPRING SONG SINGERS, SEA SIDE TRIPPERS, SNOW WHITE SPECIAL, ALBERT LADDIN, ASK A SILLY QUESTION, FIESTA FANDANGO, FORTY WINKS BEAUTY, IRON-HOT STRIKERS, PICCALILLI CIRCUS, RED HOT CINDERS, WAY OUT WEST, WHAT-HO WITHIN! is fully protected under the copyright laws of the British Commonwealth, including Canada, the United States of America, and all other countries of the Copyright Union. All rights, including professional and amateur stage productions, recitation, lecturing, public reading, motion picture, radio broadcasting, television and the rights of translation into foreign languages are strictly reserved.

ISBN 978-0-573-10013-0

www.samuelfrench-london.co.uk

www.samuelfrench.com

FOR AMATEUR PRODUCTION ENQUIRIES

UNITED KINGDOM AND WORLD
EXCLUDING NORTH AMERICA
plays@SamuelFrench-London.co.uk
020 7255 4302/01

Each title is subject to availability from Samuel French,

depending upon country of performance.

CAUTION: Professional and amateur producers are hereby warned that *ALI'S BARBARA, SPRING SONG SINGERS, SEA SIDE TRIPPERS, SNOW WHITE SPECIAL, ALBERT LADDIN, ASK A SILLY QUESTION, FIESTA FANDANGO, FORTY WINKS BEAUTY, IRON-HOT STRIKERS, PICCALILLI CIRCUS, RED HOT CINDERS, WAY OUT WEST, WHAT-HO WITHIN!* is subject to a licensing fee. Publication of this play does not imply availability for performance. Both amateurs and professionals considering a production are strongly advised to apply to the appropriate agent before starting rehearsals, advertising, or booking a theatre. A licensing fee must be paid whether the title is presented for charity or gain and whether or not admission is charged.

The professional rights in this play are controlled by Samuel French Ltd, 52 Fitzroy Street, London, W1T 5JR.

No one shall make any changes in this title for the purpose of production. No part of this book may be reproduced, stored in a retrieval system, or transmitted in any form, by any means, now known or yet to be invented, including mechanical, electronic, photocopying, recording, videotaping, or otherwise, without the prior written permission of the publisher. No one shall upload this title, or part of this title, to any social media websites.

The right of Richard Tydeman to be identified as author of this work has been asserted in accordance with Section 77 of the Copyright, Designs and Patents Act 1988.

Ali's Barbara

An Arabian Nightmare of a Minidrama

Richard Tydeman

A Samuel French Acting Edition

FOUNDED 1830

SAMUELFRENCH-LONDON.CO.UK
SAMUELFRENCH.COM

CHARACTERS

in order of appearance

THE COMPERE
ALI, *of Baghdad*
BARBARA, *his daughter*
CASSIM, *Ali's brother*
FATIMA, *Cassim's chief wife*
JASMIN, *Cassim's second wife*
ZENA, *Cassim's third wife*
SARA, *Cassim's fourth wife*
FIRST MYSTERIOUS INTRUDER
SECOND MYSTERIOUS INTRUDER
THIRD MYSTERIOUS INTRUDER
Two or more SLAVES

SCENE: Ali's house in old Baghdad.

ALI'S BARBARA

The COMPERE, *in Eastern dress, appears in front of the curtain, bows to the audience, unrolls a large scroll in which a copy of the script is concealed, and begins:—*

COMPERE. Once, long ago, in the far off days
When Arabian Nights were all the craze,
There lived in the city of old Baghdad
A bloke named Ali—a likeable lad;
He earned enough as a market porter
To keep himself and his motherless daughter,
The prettiest lass between Suez and Scarborough,
Known to her friends as Ali's Barbara.
Come then, to Ali's house with me,
As Barbara pours her dad some tea.

(Curtain rises. ALI *is reclining on a divan, while* BARBARA *pours him some tea which he drinks.* COMPERE *stands down* L.*)*

His meal complete, her father sighs
And looks his daughter in the eyes.

ALI. My daughter, I have news to tell.
COMPERE. To which the damsel answers,
BARBARA.   Well?
ALI. Your Uncle Cassim wants to stay.
COMPERE. The maid replies,
BARBARA.   That's spoilt my day.
ALI. Why, don't you like your Uncle Cassim?
BARBARA. If I could have my way, I'd gas him!
COMPERE. Which statement makes it pretty clear
That Cassim's not a favourite here.
BARBARA. His sneering ways just make me itch.
It's not our fault that we're not rich.
COMPERE. But there's no time for any more,
For someone's knocking at the door.

(Knocking is heard. BARBARA *lowers her veil and opens door.)*

And from his carriage in the street
Steps Uncle Cassim with his suite.

(Enter CASSIM, *followed by four veiled wives.)*

With unctuous smile he turns to say,

CASSIM. Well Ali, how's the world today?
COMPERE. Then next his niece's hand he grabs:

CASSIM.	And how's my darling little Babs?
	(BARBARA *turns away in disgust.*)
COMPERE.	But Cassim's wives are looking daggers,
	And all of them are frightful naggers;
	So, following their mute instructions,
	Cassim proceeds to introductions.
CASSIM.	My chief wife Fatima you've met,
	And this is Jasmin, she's a pet;
	Zena and Sara, they're both new.
	Now come on, girls, say how d'you do.
FATIMA.	Dear Barbara, what a charming smile.
	(*Aside.*) Her clothes are all in last year's style.
JASMIN.	I've heard so much about you, dear.
	(*Aside.*) And most of it was true, I fear.
ZENA.	Pleased to meet you.
SARA.	Charmed, I'm sure.
ZENA AND SARA (*together, aside*).	It must be awful to be poor.
COMPERE.	Now Barbara looks a bit askance—
	She's never had so many aunts.
	But quickly she regains the poise
	That every well-bred girl enjoys
	When facing this emergency
	And says,
BARBARA.	You'll have a cup of tea?
COMPERE.	They all say,
FOUR WIVES (*quickly*).	Yes please!
COMPERE.	Like a shot.
	The journey's made them very hot;
	But ladies cannot lift their veils
	When in the company of males.
	So with the tea-pot and the tray,
	To Barbara's room they make their way,

(BARBARA *goes out with tea tray, followed by the* FOUR WIVES.)

And leave the men a little longer
To quench their thirst with something stronger.

(CASSIM *produces a bottle of whisky and fills the cups with it.* ALI *and* CASSIM *continue to drink during the next eight lines.*)

Now just in case there's someone here
Who thinks this story's rather queer,
Allow me to explain a minute:
The Forty Thieves do not come in it;
For all this happened years before,

ALI'S BARBARA

                In what are known as "days of yore":
                So with that word of explanation,
                I'll now get back to my narration.
                The bottle's less than quarter full,
                When Cass gives Ali's sleeve a pull,
                And asks him in a voice that wavers
                If he'll do some little favours.

CASSIM (*thickly*). The Tax Collector's on my tracks,
                So with me I've brought fifty sacks . . .
                (*He mumbles into his cup of whisky.*)

COMPERE.   But as he's whispering—in his cup, too!—
                I'd better tell you what he's up to.
                One sack is full of gold and loot,
                And forty-nine are packed with fruit.
                For Cassim, as the phone-book states,
                Retails bananas, figs and dates.

CASSIM.   So be a jolly decent feller,
                And let me stuff them down your cellar.

COMPERE.   Not used to such a lot of liquor,
                Ali's brain is muddled quicker;
                But giving Cassim's hand a squeeze
                He says:

ALI.   You stuff 'em where you please.

COMPERE.   So fifty slaves with brawny backs
                Bring in the heavy bulging sacks.

(*A* SLAVE *enters carrying a sack and goes out immediately on the same side. A* SECOND SLAVE *enters with another sack and follows the first one off. Only two slaves are necessary, and they continue to enter and go out in turn—or they can walk round and round a screen—until the curtain falls. If they can have large numbers attached to their sacks, starting with "one" and working upwards each time they enter, so much the better.*)

                But though they make the work seem light,
                It looks like going on all night.
                Still, I suppose they've got to do it,
                So I suggest we leave them to it,
                And see what's happening to Babs.
                (*Calling into the wings.*)
                Right-ho then, William, close the tabs.

(CURTAIN *falls, leaving* COMPERE *outside.*)

                Now from the world of man's rough din,
                We turn to matters feminine,
                And join the ladies as they wait
                In Barbara's boudoir, tête à tête.

ALI'S BARBARA

> So please be quiet; don't make a clatter,
> Or else you'll miss the gentle chatter
> Of ladies' voices calm and still.
> Please raise the curtain softly, Bill.

(The CURTAIN rises. The divan has gone, and in its place is a window. This can either be a proper eastern window opening or just a clothes horse, standing on two chairs, with a sheet draped over the lower half. There are rugs and teacups on the floor. FATIMA and JASMIN are sitting; ZENA and SARA are standing. All are without veils. They argue raucously.)

ZENA. It is!
SARA. It isn't!
JASMIN. Oh sit down!
ZENA. I'll bet you.
SARA. How much?
ZENA. Half a crown—It's permed.
SARA. It's not; they're natural curls.
JASMIN. You're both wrong.
FATIMA. Oh be quiet, girls!
> We can't discuss our niece's hair—
> Especially when she isn't there.
COMPERE. What's this? The visitors alone?
> (We've landed in a Danger Zone!)
> Why isn't Babs upon her rug?
JASMIN (turning). She's gone to fill the water jug.

(Enter BARBARA with hot water jug.)

BARBARA. I'm sorry I've been rather long.
> How do you like it? Weak or strong?
COMPERE. So peace is now restored once more.
> And sitting down upon the floor,
> They all resume their proper station
> And join in pleasant conversation.
> But while they gaily drink their tea,
> Behind their backs they do not see
> Three stealthy figures softly creeping,
> And through the window rudely peeping.

(Enter, crawling, three men of fearsome aspect, who get behind the window and pop their heads up over the sill one at a time.)

> Three dirty double-dealers dashing;
> Their double-crossing eyes aflashing.

ALI'S BARBARA

       Three double-barrelled names they carry—
       Tom-tom, Dik-dik and Harri-harri.
       (*The men's heads disappear.*)
       Now Cassim's spouses, one by one,
       Worn out by travelling in the sun,
       Contentedly their eyes are closing,
       And very soon all four are dozing.
       (*The wives all sleep.*)
       Then Barbara rises from the floor,
       But scarcely has she reached the door,
    (*As* BARBARA *reaches door,* TOM-TOM'S *head appears at the window.*)
       When from the window comes the sound
       Of:—

TOM.   Psst!
COMPERE.   And quickly turning round,
       She strangles back a cry of fright
       At such an unexpected sight.
TOM.   Oh shrink not, maiden, in alarm,
       We do not wish you any harm.
DIK (*popping up in the window*). We all do really high-class jobs.
HARRI (*popping up between them with a fiendish grin*).
       That's right. We only murder nobs.
    (TOM-TOM *and* DIK-DIK *quickly thrust him down out of sight.*)
COMPERE.   But Barbara's puzzled by these three;
       She's in the dark—and so are we,
       Until the leader starts explaining,
       And soon her confidence he's gaining.
TOM.   You see we go from door to door,
       And rob the rich to pay the poor.
DIK.   When wealthy men we find, we woo them.
HARRI (*popping up between them*).
       And if they won't pay up, we *do* them!
    (*He draws a finger across his neck and makes a horrid noise with his throat. The others thrust him down.*)
TOM.   We hear that Cassim's near at hand,
       With fifty sacks of contraband.
DIK.   If you can help us find this wizard,
HARRI (*thrusting the other two down as he pops up brandishing an enormous knife.*) We'll cut his throat from crop to gizzard!
       (TOM-TOM *and* DIK-DIK *pull him down and reappear.*)

ALI'S BARBARA

DIK. Please take no notice of our friend,
He's definitely round the bend.
TOM. Well, will you help us in our quest?
COMPERE. Babs thinks; and then—
BARBARA. I'll do my best.
COMPERE. Now Uncle Cassim's met his match,
For Barbara starts her plans to hatch.
She tells the three to come tonight,
And knowing Cassim's short of sight,
She says:—
BARBARA. Just do your hair in curls,
And come disguised as dancing girls.
TOM. Oh what a plan!
DIK. But s'pose it fails?
HARRI (*popping up between them and speaking in a cissy voice*).
I've come without my seven veils.

(*He ducks as if expecting the others to turn on him, but they take no notice.*)

COMPERE. But now the sleeping wives awake,
So noiselessly their leave they take,
And whisper:—
TOM (*whispering*). Till tonight.
DIK (*whispering*). Farewell.
HARRI (*loudly*). We're going to give old Cassim — — —

(*The other two put their hands over his mouth and drag him off. The wives are now awake.*)

COMPERE. Well!
The ladies view Babs with suspicion,
Until she makes the bold admission:
BARBARA. Tonight we're going to have a party.
COMPERE. They all rejoice with cheerings hearty.
Then suddenly they stop and stare.
JASMIN. We haven't got a *thing* to wear!
COMPERE. But isn't that, O husbands pray,
What married ladies *always* say?
So pull the curtain, let them go
And occupy an hour or so
With paint and powder, brush and file.
The curtains, William!

(CURTAIN *falls.*)

ALI'S BARBARA

That's the style.
Now sinks the blazing sun to rest,
And darkness creeps from east to west.
The golden mantle of the day
Is folded up and put away;
And as the daylight hours are done,
The stars come peeping, one by one.
You realise of course that I'm
Just filling in a little time,
And improvising in between,
To let our stage-hands set the scene.
The silver moon with radiance bright
Is shining through the velvet night.
I hope they'll speed their preparation,
I'm running out of inspiration!

(*Turning towards curtain.*)

You're ready? Right. Then on we go
To see the last act of our show.

(CURTAIN *rises as on first scene.* BARBARA *is sitting between* ALI *and* CASSIM *on the divan. The wives are sitting on the floor, two on either side. The* SLAVES *are serving fruit and wine.*)

The shades of night have fallen fast,
And supper time is nearly past.
The wine is flowing like a river—
And Cassim's got a touch of liver.

(CASSIM *gives a hiccup.*)

But watchful Babs is wide awake,
And keeps her eyes on Dad's intake.

(SLAVE *goes to fill* ALI'S *cup, but* BARBARA *intervenes.*)

Then comes the moment she's expecting,
When Cassim, all his thoughts collecting,
Claps his hands and loudly yells:—

CASSIM (*clapping twice*). Bring in the Dancing Gels!
COMPERE.   Then amid sounds of girlish glee,
            Emerge our enterprising three.

(*Enter* TOM-TOM, DIK-DIK *and* HARRI-HARRI, *disguised as dancing girls. They perform an outlandish, eastern dance. At the end the others all clap.*)

            Says Ali, as his guests applaud:
ALI.   Ask what you please as your reward.
COMPERE.   Without delay the leading dancer
            Turns in a flash and gives an answer
            As quick as aeroplane's propeller:

ALI'S BARBARA

TOM.	We'd like one sack from down your cellar.
ALI.	I can't go back upon my word.
COMPERE.	But poor old Cassim hasn't heard.

The three rush off to choose their sack,
    (*Exeunt the three, running.*)
And presently they hurry back,
    (*They re-enter, running, with sack.*)
And dump the sack upon the floor;
  (*They drop sack which obviously contains metal.*)
Then Cassim wakes up with a roar:

CASSIM.	You can't have that! It's one of mine.
TOM.	And all the other forty-nine?
CASSIM.	Yes, yes.
COMPERE.	Disguise is at an end.

    (*The three throw off disguises.*)
The three accusing strangers bend,
With outstretched fingers.

TOM.	How d'you do?
	We're from the Inland Revenue.
DIK.	Now kindly pay the tax you owe,
HARRI.	Or into dungeons dark you go.

        (CASSIM *swoons.*)

COMPERE.	But wasted are the words they say,
	For Cassim's fainted clean away.
FATIMA.	Oh sirs, my husband's very poor—
	And five can't live as cheap as four.
JASMIN.	Have pity on his starving wives,
ZENA AND SARA	(*together*). And we will love you all our lives.
COMPERE.	At this display of female favour,
	Dik-Dik and Harri-Harri waver.

        (CASSIM *recovers.*)

DIK.	Look here, Tom-Tom, it may be rash,
	But wives would be more fun than cash.
HARRI.	I vote that Cassim we release,
	And settle for a wife apiece.
COMPERE.	At this arrangement Cass connives,

    (CASSIM *clutches his sack, nodding.*)
    He'd rather have hard cash than wives.

ALI'S BARBARA

(Dik-Dik *takes* Zena *down* l. Harri-Harri *takes* Sara *down* r.)

        The other wives to Tom-Tom run.

Fatima and Jasmin *(together).* Will you have both of us, or one?

Compere.   But Tom-Tom pushes both aside;
He has in mind another bride.
And turning now to Ali's daughter,
With glowing words he starts to court her.
For though he seeks for tax collectable,
Yet really he is quite respectable.

Tom.   I am Sultan of Avabanana.
Sweet Babs, will you be my Sultana?

Compere.   The maiden blushes, gives a start,
And then says:

Barbara.   Yes, with all my heart.

Ali.   Hey, just a minute, Sultan, sir,
I cannot manage without her.
If you take Babs, what *shall* I do?

Cassim.   Have one of mine; I've still got tw

(*So* Ali *takes* Jasmin, *leaving* Fatima *for* Cassim.)

Compere.   So thus we solve a tricky question
Without hard words or indigestion.
We've paired them off, and just in time—
The way they do in pantomime.
It's time to draw the curtain now,
So forward please, and take your bow.

(*They come forward in couples, bow and step back again.*)

        The moral of our little show
Is obvious to all, I know:—
You husbands, have you noisy wives?
And do they aggravate your lives,
And wear the trousers in your shacks?
Then pay them as your Income Tax!
Send every hen who is a pecker
To the Chancellor of the Exchequer.
Thus all your troubles will come right;
And we wish you a Good—Arabian—Night.

Curtain

Spring Song Singers

A Minidrama

Richard Tydeman

A Samuel French Acting Edition

FOUNDED 1830

SAMUELFRENCH-LONDON.CO.UK
SAMUELFRENCH.COM

SPRING SONG SINGERS

A minidrama in atrocious prose, for ten or more characters of either sex, with opportunities to insert additional local matter. Easy to learn, easy to stage and requiring very few rehearsals.

CHARACTERS

The Hall Cleaner
The Cleaner's Friend
The Conductor
The Singers (*any number, good, bad or preferably indifferent*)
The Pianist, *who only strikes one chord*!

Scene : The hall where the entertainment is taking place, early in the evening

PRODUCTION NOTE

Spring Song Singers has been specially written for quick learning and easy staging and requires few rehearsals. Many opportunities are given for the players to insert topical, local and personal patter and business, ad.lib., and these opportunities, when fully used, will add considerably to the fun of the piece, bringing its length nearly up to half-an-hour.

Although the piece is about a choir, no singing is included, and the Pianist only has to play a chord on the piano, so that the whole thing can be performed by people with no musical knowledge whatever.
If, however, the Singers really are singers, the ending could be altered and the Conductor could decide to practise the music for tomorrow after all. The piece would then finish with some genuine singing.

It is suggested that each Singer should have a copy with a bold design on the front, possibly bearing the name "Spring Song Singers" at the top. This would draw attention to Singer Two's copy when it is held upside-down. Each music copy should contain a copy of the words as well!

The "key tied to the chair leg" should really be kept concealed in the Cleaner's hand until the moment comes when it is "found". It is unwise to tie it to any particular chair in case the chair really does get moved!

Producers will arrange the Singers how they like, but a workable arrangement is as follows : Front row, seated L to R, Singers 3,6, 5,7,12,1. Back row standing, Singers 2,10,11,4,9,8. These are their original positions; afterwards of course Singers 2 and 3 change places.

If twelve Singers are not available the parts may be doubled, each player taking two of the parts as written. A workable arrangement would then be as follows : Front row, the players taking 2 and 12, 9 and 11, 1 and 7. Back row, 6 and 10, 4 and 5, 3 and 7. If more than twelve Singers are available, increase both rows, or make a third row and invent lines in the "ad.lib." sections for the additional players.

Only the Cleaner and the Conductor have more than 12 lines to learn and if necessary the Conductor could have a copy of the words concealed amongst the music on his stand, thus acting a prompter as well. The Cleaner could conceal a copy in a bucket or duster.

The piece can equally well be performed by all men, all women or a mixed cast, and be equally atrocious either way!

Richard Tydeman

SPRING SONG SINGERS

The curtains — if any — are open and half-a-dozen chairs are on the stage or platform. The piano, on or near the stage, is closed. No other furniture, stage-setting or effects required.

The CLEANER *enters from the back of the hall, with bucket and cleaning implements, followed by the* CLEANER'S FRIEND.

CLEANER. Come on in, and shut the door behind you.

FRIEND *(looking round critically).* Coo, is this the . . . Hall? *(Insert the name of the hall, hut or room, where the performance is being held.)*

CLEANER *(getting on the stage).* Yes.

FRIEND. Blimey.

CLEANER. Why, what's the matter with it?

FRIEND. It's a bit small, isn't it? *(Or "a bit large", depending on size of hall.)*

(Ad lib. conversation, with FRIEND *making disparaging comments on the various peculiarities of the Hall — imaginary or otherwise: e.g. "those hard chairs . . ." "the heating system . . . " "them poky little windows" etc. The* CLEANER *replies dolefully, each time.)*

CLEANER. Yes, I know.

FRIEND. Well, I don't envy you your job. Do you have much trouble?

CLEANER. Trouble? It's all trouble. People behave in this hall like they never would at home.

FRIEND. Go on?

CLEANER. Well, take them dances they have. Next morning it's fag-ends on me floor, chewing-gum on me chairbacks, and dust all over me dado.

(Ad lib. conversation in which CLEANER *magnifies the faults of the various users of the hall: e.g. "The scouts light fires on me floor-polish . . ." "The cubs camp out in me kitchen . . ." "The Sunday school stick stamps on me stucco . . ." "The whist drives . . ." "The women's meetings . . ." etc., etc., to each of which the* FRIEND *replies)*

FRIEND. Go on?

CLEANER. Of course, you'll keep all this to yourself, won't you?

FRIEND. Oh yes.

CLEANER. It's a good thing the hall is empty now; I shouldn't like anyone else to hear this conversation.

FRIEND. Coo, no.

CLEANER. Specially the . . . *(Here insert the name of any organisation widely represented in the audience.)* they're the worst of the lot! *(Continue ad lib. until this topic is exhausted.)*

SPRING SONG SINGERS

CLEANER. Well, I'd better make a start on scrubbing me stage.
(Enter, from back of hall, the CONDUCTOR, *followed by the* SINGERS — *any number from six upwards. All carry music.)*
CONDUCTOR. Ah yes, there's somebody about. Good. Follow me, all of you. Last one close the door.
CLEANER. Hullo, hullo, what's all this?
CONDUCTOR *(advancing to front)*. Good evening: This is the . . . hall?
CLEANER. Yes, that's right.
CONDUCTOR. Good. We are the Spring Song Singers.
CLEANER. You're a bit previous, aren't you?
CONDUCTOR. We wanted to get a practice in.
CLEANER *(doubtfully)*. Oh.
CONDUCTOR. It's quite all right, we have seen the vicar. *(Or insert the name of the person responsible for letting the hall.)*
CLEANER. Oh well, that's different. He never told me of course, but then, nobody never tells me nothing. I'm always the last one to hear.
CONDUCTOR. We can have our practice then?
CLEANER. I suppose so. I *was* going to scrub me stage but you'll just have to stand in your own dirt, that's all. *(To* FRIEND.*)* Come on, we'll go and sit at the back and listen.
   *(*CLEANER *and* FRIEND *go to back of hall and sit.)*
CONDUCTOR. Now Singers, to your places please.
      *(*SINGERS *take up positions on the stage. Numbers are unimportant but if there are about a dozen, six should sit in a row on chairs, and the other six stand behind them.* CONDUCTOR *unfolds and erects a portable music-stand and sorts out music.)*
SINGER ONE *(rubbing finger on chair and looking at it)*. This chair is terribly dusty.
CLEANER *(from back of hall)*. I can hear you!
SINGER ONE. Well, it *is*.
CLEANER. Of course it is. I haven't had a chance to do any cleaning up there yet. *(To* FRIEND.*)* I can see we're in for trouble with this lot.
SINGER TWO *(who has got pushed into the back row)*. I am afraid I can't stand here all the evening; my doctor says I must sit down as much as possible. Could someone in the front row change places with me?
(The front row stare stonily ahead.)
If someone would be so kind?
(No one moves. SINGER TWO *suddenly points dramatically at the floor at the front of the stage.)*
Oh! Is that a mouse?
(Front row jump up with cries of alarm. SINGER TWO *promptly sits on one of the now empty chairs.)*
Oh no, it's only a bit of fluff. What a relief. Oh, I've come over all faint.

SPRING SONG SINGERS

(*Fans self with music. Front row, making disapproving comments, resume seats — all except* SINGER THREE *whose chair is now occupied by* SINGER TWO.)
SINGER THREE. Here! You've taken my seat!
    (SINGER TWO *is too faint to reply and continues fanning with closed eyes.*)
Hey, you.
CONDUCTOR (*who has now finished sorting music*). Now now, come come. If you please, Singers, if you please.
SINGER THREE. My seat!
CONDUCTOR. I beg your pardon?
SINGER THREE. My seat, my seat!
CONDUCTOR. What's the matter with it?
SINGER THREE. It's been pinched.
CONDUCTOR. Don't be facetious, please. Now we must get on. I can't have anyone standing in front you know. Take your place behind the chairs please. Quickly!
    (SINGER THREE *moves into the back row, muttering.*)
Now we'll start with our Spring Song Singers' signature tune. Is our accompanist ready?
SINGER FOUR. She (*Or he.*) isn't here yet.
CONDUCTOR. Not here? Not here? Why not?
SINGER FOUR. There was some difficulty about parking the car.
CONDUCTOR. Well, we *must* make a start. Can anyone else play the piano? (*To* SINGER FIVE.) What about you?
SINGER FIVE. Me? Oh no, I couldn't.
SINGER SIX (*next to* SINGER FIVE). Yes you could.
SINGER FIVE. No no, really.
SINGER SIX. Oh go on, you know you can.
SINGER FIVE. I can't.
SINGER SIX. You can.
SINGER FIVE. No, no. What about you?
SINGER SIX. Me? Oh no, I don't play.
SINGER FIVE. Yes you do, you know you do.
SINGER SIX. Not well enough for that.
SINGER FIVE. Have a try.
SINGER SIX. Oh no; not with you here.
SINGER FIVE. I'm not good enough.
    (*This can go on ad lib., with others joining in and taking sides, until all the* SINGERS *are talking at once. Eventually the* CONDUCTOR *claps and shouts to restore order.*)
CONDUCTOR. Please, *please*, PLEASE! (*Silence.*) That's better.
SINGER SEVEN (*a quiet, inoffensive little* SINGER *on the front row, succumbing to hiccoughs.*) Hic.
CONDUCTOR. I beg your pardon?
SINGER SEVEN. Granted — I mean — hic.
CONDUCTOR. Try holding your breath.
    (*Ad lib. conversation, in which everybody contributes their*

own pet remedy for hiccoughs: e.g. "putting your head between your knees . . ." "breathing into a paper bag . . ." "drinking water from the wrong side of the glass . . ." "getting someone to frighten you . . ." *etc. Others could contribute gloomy reminiscences of people they have known who have died from hiccoughs, etc. Eventually:)*

CONDUCTOR. Yes, yes, this is all very interesting, but we must get on. Now then, who is going to play the piano?

SINGER FIVE
SINGER SIX } *(together).* I am.

CONDUCTOR. You can't both play.

SINGER FIVE *(to* SINGER SIX*).* Well, I don't mind, if you'd rather.

SINGER SIX. No, no; you spoke first.

SINGER FIVE. Oh, I didn't.

SINGER SIX. Yes you did.

SINGER FIVE. But I'd rather . . .

(Etc., etc. CONDUCTOR *eventually shouts again.)*

CONDUCTOR. PLEASE!

(Silence.)

SINGER SEVEN. Hic.

CONDUCTOR. Well, we shall just have to sing unaccompanied then.

(Enter, from back of hall, the PIANIST, *a short-sighted, nervous type, carrying sheaves of music which keep dropping and have to be picked up by* CLEANER, FRIEND *and* SINGERS.*)*

PIANIST. Excuse me, excuse me. Thank you. Oh dear, I've dropped it. Would you mind? Thank you. Oh dear, there's another one. Thank you. Excuse me, thank you. *(Reaching* CONDUCTOR.*)* Oh, here you are. I thought I should never find you. I had to find a safe place to park my little car. It's not easy these days, is it? Have I dropped something? Oh thank you. *(Etc.)*

CONDUCTOR. Now you've arrived we can start. We are opening with our signature tune.

PIANIST *(sorting music on top of piano).* Signature tune, ah yes. Signature tune. Let me see, what's this? "Monastery Garden", no. "Nymphs and Shepherds", no. "Flat Foot Boogie", no. Ah, here it is, yes, the signature tune.

CONDUCTOR. Will you give us a chord?

PIANIST. Certainly, certainly, just let me — *(Attempts to open keyboard lid, but it will not open.)* Oh dear.

CONDUCTOR. What's the matter?

PIANIST. It's locked up.

CONDUCTOR. Oh good heavens. Now what do we do?

SINGER EIGHT *(bright and brainless).* I expect there would be a key somewhere.

CONDUCTOR. Say that again.

SINGER EIGHT. A key. There usually is, you know.

CONDUCTOR. This week's most intelligent comment. *(Shouting.)* Of course there's a key somewhere! But where?

SPRING SONG SINGERS

SINGER NINE. Why not ask that caretaker person.
CLEANER *(from back of hall)*. Don't you call me a person. I won't have language like that in my hall!
SINGER NINE. Oh, I'm sorry. I didn't mean to offend.
CONDUCTOR. Please, please, please. *(To* CLEANER.*)* Now, could you kindly let us have the key to the piano?
CLEANER. It's tied to the chair-leg.
CONDUCTOR. Which chair-leg?
CLEANER. The chair by the piano.

(PIANIST *and others turn the chair over, but find no key.*)

PIANIST. It's not here.
CLEANER. It must be. Oh, I know what's happened, they've gone and shifted all the chairs round again. Why can't people leave things alone?
CONDUCTOR. Which chair is the key on then?
CLEANER. I don't know. It might be on any of the chairs in this hall. I'll have a look. *(To* FRIEND.*)* Here, you can help.

(SINGERS *look under their chairs.* CLEANER *and* FRIEND *search under audience's chairs. Eventually the key is found.*)

Here it is. Here it is. *(Key is passed up to* PIANIST.*)*
PIANIST. Oh thank you, thank you.

(PIANIST *opens keyboard and sits.*)

CONDUCTOR. At last! Now, is everybody ready? Chord please.

(PIANIST *plays a chord.* CONDUCTOR *raises baton. All* SINGERS *open their music copies and hold them up.* SINGER TWO'S *copy is upside down.* CONDUCTOR *notices this and lowers baton, clearing throat loudly.*)

Ahem, ahem!

(The others lower their music and look at SINGER TWO, *who continues to hold copy upside down.* CONDUCTOR *goes closer and taps copy.)*

SINGER TWO *(lowering copy)*. What is it?
CONDUCTOR. Are you with us?
SINGER TWO. Certainly.
CONDUCTOR. Do you usually read music upside down?
SINGER TWO. Oh, is it upside down? I forgot to bring my glasses.
CONDUCTOR *(raises clenched fists to the sky)*. You forgot to bring your glasses! Heaven grant me patience!
SINGER TEN *(back row)*. Would you care to borrow mine? *(Offers glasses to* SINGER TWO.*)*
SINGER TWO. Oh, how kind. Are you sure you can spare them?
SINGER TEN. Yes, yes. I don't need them for reading.

(Ad lib. conversation in which different SINGERS *tell how they only wear glasses for walking, cooking, driving the car, playing cards, eating grapefruit, etc.)*

CONDUCTOR *(eventually, with heavy sarcasm)*. When you are all ready — when you are all *quite* ready . . .

SPRING SONG SINGERS

SINGER TEN *(to* SINGER TWO*).* Do try them on.
SINGER TWO *(putting on glasses).* Oh, what an extraordinary effect: I can see two conductors! No, that won't do. *(Hands glasses back.)*
CONDUCTOR *(raising baton).* How many conductors can you see now?
SINGER TWO. Oh, only one now.
CONDUCTOR *(dangerously quiet).* Good. Can you all see me?
SINGERS. Yes.
CONDUCTOR. Can you see my baton raised?
SINGERS. Yes.
CONDUCTOR. And do you know what that means? It means we are ready to begin — *(Shouting.)* — ready to begin. Do you hear?
SINGER ELEVEN *(taking umbrage).* Well really! There's no need to shout like that.
    (While this is going on, the CLEANER *opens the door at the back and goes out to talk to someone outside.)*
CONDUCTOR. Are you ready?
SINGER ELEVEN. Ready? Of course we're ready. We've been ready for the last ten minutes. I didn't join this choir just to be insulted. If we are going to be spoken to like this, I am going home.
CONDUCTOR. My dear madam, *(Or sir.)* you are only wasting what little time we have. If we don't get our practice in before the audience arrive, we shall get no practice at all. Now, are you ready?
SINGER ELEVEN *(subsiding).* Well, really! . . .
CONDUCTOR. The chord again please. (PIANIST *repeats chord.)* Now. The Spring Song Singers' signature tune. I shall give you two beats and you come in on "three". Right. One two . . .
CLEANER *(from door at back of hall).* Just a minute.
CONDUCTOR *(turning).* Yes, yes, what is it now?
CLEANER. There's a policeman outside.
CONDUCTOR. A policeman?
CLEANER. He wants a word with the owner of a small grey Morris that's parked the wrong way round on a pedestrian crossing with no lights on.
    (PIANIST *drops keyboard lid with a crash and looks terribly guilty. All gaze at* PIANIST.)
PIANIST. I'm afraid it's probably mine.
CONDUCTOR. Well, you'd better go quickly.
PIANIST. Er — yes.
    (PIANIST *shuffles and sidles off platform, down hall and out. All watch in awed silence till door closes.)*
CONDUCTOR. *Now* what's to be done?
SINGER FOUR. About six months I should think.
    (All stare at SINGER FOUR *who subsides.)*
CONDUCTOR. You realise that we shall now have to sing the entire programme without a pianist?

SPRING SONG SINGERS

SINGER EIGHT *(brightly).* Then I suggest we should sing unaccompanied instead.

(CONDUCTOR *leans against platform and covers face with hands.*)

CONDUCTOR *(eventually, looking at watch).* Singers, the time by my watch is six-forty-five. By seven-fifteen this hall will be half full of audience arriving for the concert. We have about twenty-five minutes. *(With rising voice.)* Do you want a practice, or don't you?

SINGER TWELVE *(consulting watch).* I think you are a bit slow.

CONDUCTOR *(angrily).* What was that remark?

SINGER TWELVE. I said I think you are a bit slow. My watch says seven-fifteen now.

CONDUCTOR. What?

(*The* SINGERS *all consult their watches and, although their times all disagree:* "Mine says seven-fourteen and a half . . ." "It's exactly sixteen minutes past by the wireless . . ." "Mine was two minutes slow at one o'clock but it gains a minute every six hours . . ." "I'm never wrong . . ." *etc., it appears that it is certainly about seven-fifteen.*)

SINGER TWELVE *(triumphantly).* You see, you must be slow.

CONDUCTOR *(holding watch to ear).* My watch has stopped. Well then, that settles it. We haven't got time to practise at all.

SINGER ONE. But surely — I mean — if it is really quarter past seven now, where are the audience?

CONDUCTOR *(gazing down hall).* Audience? Yes, where *are* the audience? *(To* CLEANER.*)* Here, you, Caretaker.

CLEANER *(who was in deep conversation with* FRIEND*).* Are you calling me?

CONDUCTOR. Is there anyone waiting outside?

CLEANER. Outside? *(Opens door and looks.)* No. Why?

CONDUCTOR. Extraordinary. This *is* the . . . hall?

CLEANER. Course it is.

CONDUCTOR. I presume *some* tickets were sold for this concert?

CLEANER. Oh yes, any amount. I bought one myself.

CONDUCTOR. Then where are the audience?

CLEANER *(coming to front, followed by* FRIEND*).* The audience?

CONDUCTOR. The concert starts at half past seven, doesn't it?

CLEANER. Yes, half past seven tomorrow.

ALL. Tomorrow!

CLEANER. Why yes. Didn't you know?

(*Ad lib. consternation, and cries of* "Why weren't we told? . . ." "I can't possibly come tomorrow . . ." "Bad organisation . . ." "Sack the conductor . . ." *etc., leading on to further cries of* "Come on, let's go home . . ." "Wasting our time like this . . ." *etc., as* SINGERS *file off down hall and out.* CONDUCTOR *goes last, practically tearing hair.*)

FRIEND *(when they have gone).* They are a rum lot, aren't they?

CLEANER. Barmy, if you ask me. (*They move on to the platform.*) Oh well, now they're out of the way, I can get on and scrub me stage. Pull them curtains across, will you? It'll keep the draught off. (FRIEND *moves to do so.*) Here, I say, do you want a ticket for a concert tomorrow night? You can have mine if you like. I'm going to stay at home and watch the telly — it *can't* be worse than this!

CURTAIN

Sea Side Trippers

A Minidrama

Richard Tydeman

A Samuel French Acting Edition

FOUNDED 1830

SAMUELFRENCH-LONDON.CO.UK
SAMUELFRENCH.COM

Characters

The Announcer
The Oldest Resident
The Second Oldest Resident
The Trippers, including The Young One, The
    Informative One, The Cheery One, The
    Gloomy One, The Anxious One, The
    Knitter, The Mother, The President, The
    Secretary, The Adventurous One, The
    Hungry One and The Reader

Scene: A secluded bay on the sea-coast, just before lunch

In response to the request of many teams for a successor to the same author's *Spring Song Singers*, this minidrama has been written in similar style, for the same selection of characters, and is just as easy to learn and produce, but it is in no sense a sequel and is quite complete in itself. Only two people have more than twelve lines - and one of those has a book!

SEA SIDE TRIPPERS

The scene represents a secluded bay on the sea-coast. The backcloth or back wall of the stage represents cliffs; the stage is the beach; the footlights mark the water's edge, and the audience is in the sea. Up R. *are some high rocks and in front of them some low rocks.* L. *is a single low rock. These rocks consist of tables, chairs and boxes, covered with black or coloured cloths.*

Down R. *in a deck chair sits the* OLDEST RESIDENT. *Down* L., *in another deck chair, sits the* SECOND OLDEST RESIDENT. *They are turned away from the audience, wrapped in rugs, etc., with sunshades or canopies or newspapers to hide their heads. They are both fast asleep.*

Before the curtain rises, THE ANNOUNCER *appears before the curtain—or the* ANNOUNCER'S *voice can be heard over the theatre's loudspeakers.*

ANNOUNCER (*in the exaggerated style of the introduction to an American travel film*). Come with me now to a beautiful and secluded little bay on the sea coast of sunny England. (*Or, of course,* sunny Scotland, Wales, Jersey, Tasmania, *or where you like.*)

(*The Curtain rises.*)

Far from the noisy roar of the mighty city, the two oldest residents from the exclusive Guest House enjoy the quiet beauty of a summer's day. Above them the mighty cliffs afford shelter from the wayward wind. Around them stand old and weather-beaten rocks; beneath them lies the sand and shingle beach; and you, my friends, are all, of course, under the sea.

Let us pause awhile and contemplate the beauties of this lovely, lonely, fascinating spot. (*Exit.*)

OLDEST RESIDENT (*waking up and leaning out of chair*). I say. (*Pause.*) Er—I say. Oh well, if you are asleep it doesn't matter. (*Settles back and goes to sleep.*)
SECOND OLDEST RESIDENT (*stirring sleepily after a pause*). Eh? What was that? (*Looking round.*) I thought somebody said something. (*Goes to sleep again.*)
OLDEST RESIDENT (*stirring after a pause*). Ah, you've woken up, have you? (*Leans across.*) I was only going to say—(*No movement from the other.*) Oh well, it doesn't matter. (*Goes to sleep again.*)
(*Enter up* L., *the first of the* TRIPPERS, THE YOUNG ONE, *who looks all round, then beckons off stage and calls.*)
YOUNG. Oo—oo! Everybody! Come down here; there's a lovely bit of sand. Oh come on! There's only a couple of—(*Breaks off and looks intently at the two in the deck chairs.*) there's only a couple

of old geysers fast asleep. Mind how you come down the path, it's a bit slippery. Throw some of the things down; I'll catch them. Ready now.

(Various bundles are thrown on from up L., apparently from further up the cliff. Coats, towels, bathing costumes, brown paper parcels, beach balls, cushions and rugs—the more the merrier. The YOUNG ONE *comments on these ad lib., as they arrive.)*

Is that the lot?

(Turns and bends over the heap. A final bundle—perhaps a rolled up mattress or large cushion, knocks YOUNG ONE *on to the heap.)*

Hey!

(Enter several of the TRIPPERS, *up L. In spite of the things thrown down, they are all heavily laden with bags, baskets, coats, umbrellas, stools, etc. First to enter are* THE INFORMATIVE ONE, THE CHEERY ONE *and* THE GLOOMY ONE, *followed by* THE ANXIOUS ONE *and* THE KNITTER.*)*

INFORMATIVE *(moving down R.).* Ah, this is the little cove that the Guide Book mentions. Now where did I see it? *(Turns pages of guide book.)*

CHEERY *(moving down L.).* Well, here we are at the seaside at last. *(Looking round.)* Ooh, isn't it lovely!

GLOOMY *(L.C.).* We should have done better to go to Clacton. *(Or "Blackpool" or some other well-known resort.)*

INFORMATIVE. We went there last year, and you complained because of the crowds.

KNITTER *(mounting high rock and sitting, counting stitches on an enormous piece of knitting).* 34, 35, 36, 37 . . .

ANXIOUS *(up C.)* Oh dear, do you think it's going to rain?

INFORMATIVE *(reading from guide book).* This particular part of the coast is noted for its humid atmosphere and has a high average rainfall.

CHEERY. Rain? Of course it won't rain. It never rains on the Club Outing. *(For "Club" insert the name of any organisation widely represented in the audience.)*

GLOOMY. Huh! Two years ago at Skegness *(Or where you like.)* we got soaked to the skin, *(To* INFORMATIVE.*)* didn't we?

INFORMATIVE *(doubtfully).* Yes, only technically that wasn't the Club Outing, it was the Institute *(Or some other organisation.),* and it was Cleethorpes not Skegness, and it was three years ago, not two.

KNITTER. 53, 54, 55, 56 . . .

CHEERY *(gazing out over audience).* Just look at the sea, sparkling away in the sunshine, and as smooth as a millpond. Who's coming to have a paddle?

ANXIOUS. Oh dear, is it safe, do you think?

GLOOMY. Wasn't it about here that those two men got sucked under by the current last summer?

ANXIOUS (*drawing back*). Oh, was it?
GLOOMY (*with relish*). They only recovered one of the bodies. (ANXIOUS *squeals.*) Isn't that right?
INFORMATIVE. Yes, only of course it was a bit further up the coast, and there were four of them, and it was in the great storm in January.
GLOOMY (*to* ANXIOUS). There you are, you see.
KNITTER. 78, 79, 80, 81 . . .
INFORMATIVE (*reading*). From the beach it is possible to obtain views of the distant islands. On a clear day when visibility is good—
YOUNG (*coming down* C.). Oh, look at that ship.
ALL. Where? Where?
YOUNG (*pointing out over audience*). There. You can only just see it. It's going over the horizon.
ANXIOUS. Is it sinking?
YOUNG. Of course not. (*Sits on floor down* R.)
GLOOMY. You can't tell. I wouldn't go over that horizon for a fortune.
CHEERY. Why not?
GLOOMY. You're all right going up the hill this side of it, because you can always turn round and come back; but once you get over the brow, you slip down the other side with nothing to stop you.
INFORMATIVE. Oh no, no, I must correct you there. Technically—
GLOOMY (*turning away*). I must sit down. My doctor warned me not to stand too long or I might have another of my turns. I don't want you lot carrying me up the cliff in a blanket; you might do me more harm than good. (*Sits on high rock, near* KNITTER, *and writes postcards.*)
KNITTER. 107, 108, 109 . . .
CHEERY. Well, I'm going to have a paddle. (*Sits on small rock* L., *and takes shoes off.*)
INFORMATIVE (*reading*). In the rock pools one may discover crabs, welks, shrimps, and even an occasional jellyfish. (*Sits on low rock* R.)
MOTHER (*off*). Oo—oo! Is this the way down?
YOUNG. Yes, come on; it's lovely.
ANXIOUS. Oh dear, it's that Mrs. Whatsit, with those two awful children. (*Sits by* CHEERY *on rock* L.)
CHEERY. Well, why not? It's their outing as much as ours.
INFORMATIVE. There I would disagree. Technically the outing is a Club Outing, and children are allowed to come only as a special concession.
YOUNG. Well, they are coming, anyway.
(*Enter* THE MOTHER, *up* L., *with two imaginary children*—"GEORGIE" *and* "JACQUELINE".)
MOTHER. Come along you two. Here we are at the seaside, and if you can't stop quarrelling I'll bang your heads together. Now go

and play on your own. Go on, Mummy doesn't want you; she just wants to sit down and have a rest.
INFORMATIVE. Come and sit here, if you like.
MOTHER. Thank you. (Sits by INFORMATIVE, on low rock R.) Georgie, take your shoes and socks off if you want to paddle. You help him Jacqueline, you're big enough. (To the others.) Cor, talk about helpless kids!
KNITTER. 121, 122, 123 . . .
CHEERY. I must say, I like children myself.
MOTHER. You're welcome to mine, any day.
INFORMATIVE. Of course, families in these days are not really big enough, you know. I was one of seven, and we never quarrelled.
ANXIOUS. There were four of us.
YOUNG. I think three is the best number, myself.
INFORMATIVE. Well, let's just take a vote on the ideal number for a family. You say three, I say seven. What about you?
MOTHER. I say two is too many.
ANXIOUS. I shall say four.
INFORMATIVE (to KNITTER). What do you say?
KNITTER. 137 . . .
INFORMATIVE. Oh, she's hopeless. (To MOTHER.) Where's everybody else gone?
MOTHER. They are round the corner in the next bay; the bus driver said we could go down either way. (Calling.) Georgie, put that seaweed down! . . . All right, sit over there and pop the little bladders if you want to, but don't wave it about.
INFORMATIVE (looking up cliff path). Here come some more of them. Oh, it's the President (Or "Chairman," "Leader," "Her Ladyship," etc.) and the Secretary.
CHEERY. There now, and I've just got my shoes and stockings off. Well, never mind, we are supposed to be enjoying ourselves.
(Enter the PRESIDENT and the SECRETARY, up L.)
PRESIDENT. Ah, there you are. (Coming down C., and looking round.) What a delightful spot.
SECRETARY (coming down C., and taking a camera from a case). Pretty. Very pretty.
PRESIDENT (indicating the two OLDEST RESIDENTS). Are these—er—
INFORMATIVE. We found them here.
PRESIDENT (whispering). Oh, really.
INFORMATIVE. You needn't whisper; they are fast asleep.
PRESIDENT. Poor dear things. I wonder how old they are?
KNITTER. 155, 156 . . .
PRESIDENT. Surely not!—Oh, I see, you've brought some work with you.
(KNITTER nods without looking up.)
SECRETARY. Now I'd just like to take a few snaps. Whereabouts is the sun? (Manoeuvres round, squinting upwards, to get best position.)

SEA SIDE TRIPPERS

MOTHER. Jacqueline! *(Louder.)* Jack-er-leen, mind what you're doing! . . . Well, if you wet them, you'll have to go home without any, because that's the only pair you've got. *(They all look at her.)* I only bought her those shoes last week.

SECRETARY *(aiming camera at audience).* Now first of all, one of the sea. *(Gazing out intently.)* Oh look, look, there's a porpoise.

ALL *(peering eagerly).* Where? Where?

SECRETARY. It's gone for the moment. Oh, I haven't seen a porpoise for years. There it is again; it looks just like an old man with a bald head.

PRESIDENT *(disapprovingly).* It *is* an old man with a bald head.

SECRETARY. Oh, so it is. Never mind. *(Takes photo.)* There; that's got one picture. *(Turns film on.)* Now one of the cliff.

MOTHER. Georgie! Come here. Where's your handkerchief? . . . On the bus? What's the use of leaving it up there? All right, you'd better use mine. *(Produces large hanky.)* Don't touch it with sandy fingers; here, blow. *(Leans towards audience, takes imaginary child's nose in handkerchief and wipes it.)* That's better. Run along.

KNITTER. 174, 175, 176 . . .

INFORMATIVE. How about taking a picture of *us,* while you are about it?

SECRETARY. Oh yes, indeed, I want to. *(Takes one of cliff and turns film on.)* I think that good snaps are the most important part of an outing, don't you?

GLOOMY. *Good* ones, yes.

PRESIDENT. Hullo, I didn't see you over there. What are you doing?

GLOOMY. Writing my postcards.

PRESIDENT. What a lot of them. Do you send them to all your friends?

GLOOMY. Not my friends, no, I send them to my neighbours; it makes them jealous.

MOTHER. Hullo, here comes trouble again. Well Jacqueline, what do you want now? . . . Well, you should have gone when everyone else did . . . All right then, get behind those bushes. *(To others.)* It always affects her like that when she puts her feet into cold water.

SECRETARY. Now could I have everybody together in a little group, please? *(They all start to form group in front of high rock R.)* That's right. *(To* PRESIDENT.*)* Would you sit in the middle? Thank you. *(They shuffle into position.)* And will you come a bit further this way . . . *(Etc., ad lib.)* Right, that should do well.

INFORMATIVE. Did you remember to turn the film on?

SECRETARY. Oh. Did I? I don't know. Yes, I think I did. I'm not sure. Number one was the sea; number two was the cliff; this should be number three. *(Examining camera.)* Let's see now, it says number—

KNITTER. 201, 202 . . .

SEA SIDE TRIPPERS

SECRETARY. No, we're all right, it says number three. Now, are we ready?
MOTHER. Half a tick. *(Calling.)* Jacqueline, hurry up. Georgie, come here. Now sit down here in front of me, and if either of you move I'll crown you.
SECRETARY *(peering into camera sight)*. Can you get any closer together? *(They try, without success.)* Well, I shall have to get further away then. *(Walks backwards, getting nearer to the edge of the stage.)*
ANXIOUS. Mind! You're walking into the sea!

(ALL *give a shriek as* SECRETARY *obviously gets feet wet.*)

SECRETARY. There now, I've got my feet wet. Oh how cold it is! Whatever shall I do?
MOTHER *(threateningly)*. Jacqueline, I've told you not to use that word. It's rude.
INFORMATIVE *(to* SECRETARY*)*. Get your shoes off quickly. Who's got a towel? *(Someone produces a towel.)* That's right; now rub your feet hard. The shoes will soon dry in the sun. Borrow these plimsols.
ANXIOUS. But what about the photograph?
INFORMATIVE. I suggest we take a group of everybody together, when we get back to the bus. And now let's have our sandwiches, shall we? It must be lunch time.

(ALL *agree, get packets from their belongings, open them and hand them round—*" ... have one of mine ...," " ... these are egg ...," " ... I made these sausage rolls myself ...," " ... I never eat meat at all ..." *Etc., ad lib.)*

I tell you what: shall we pool all our sandwiches together and then help ourselves from the pool?

(General assent—" ... good idea ...," " ... much nicer ...," " ... makes it more interesting ..." etc. MOTHER *slaps the imaginary* GEORGIE *with an* "Oh no, you don't!" *etc. They pile all the food into the lid of a large cardboard box.)*

That's the idea.
YOUNG. I say, what about the others?
INFORMATIVE. What others?
YOUNG. There should be three more of the party somewhere.
PRESIDENT. Oh yes, they are round in the next bay.
CHEERY. Well, we've got their sandwiches in this lot, so we hadn't better start until they get here.
INFORMATIVE. Let's all go and find them, shall we?
CHEERY. Good idea; and I've got a little bottle of something in the bus. We can collect that on the way. *(Slips shoes on.* ALL *prepare to go.)*
INFORMATIVE. Somebody had better stay and look after the coats and things.
CHEERY. And the sandwiches.

INFORMATIVE *(to* MOTHER*).* Would you like to stay? I'm sure the children would rather play on the beach than come for a walk.
MOTHER. Yes, I'll stay and mind the things. Off you go, all of you, but don't be too long, will you?
INFORMATIVE. No, no, we'll just go to the top of the cliff and call them. Come along everybody.
KNITTER *(as they go).* 289, 290, 291, 292 . . .
 (Exeunt up L. *all except* MOTHER, *who gets comfortably settled, and then suddenly starts up, looking off* R.*)*
MOTHER. Georgie, come down off that rock. You can't get down? You'll get down quick enough when I reach you, my lad. No, don't you move, Mummy's coming. *(Goes out* R.*)*
ADVENTUROUS ONE *(off).* Hullo! Where are you?
 (Enter down L., *the* ADVENTUROUS ONE, *the* HUNGRY ONE *and the* READER, *all in bare feet—or beach shoes—and carrying shoes and stockings with other luggage. The* HUNGRY ONE *is eating an apple, and the* READER *is reading a book.)*
Well I'm blest, they're not here at all.
HUNGRY. No, but they've left their things here, so they must be coming back. Let's sit down a bit.
 (They sit, ADVENTUROUS *on rock* R., HUNGRY *on ground* C., READER *on rock* L.*)*
I reckon we took a big risk coming round the bottom of that cliff, didn't we?
ADVENTUROUS. Oh, I don't know; the tide's still going out. *(To* READER.*)* Don't you ever stop reading?
READER. Eh? Oh, I'm sorry, I was just finishing a story—it's very exciting.
ADVENTUROUS. Go on then, read us a bit.
READER *(reading).* Slowly his cool hand crept round her warm shoulders and the hot blood surged through her icy veins. His fiery breath stirred the flaming curls on her snowy neck, and the next moment his burning kisses engulfed her frozen lips.
HUNGRY. Ooh! It makes me go hot and cold all over.
ADVENTUROUS. Just a minute. *(Gets up and examines* OLDEST RESIDENTS, *and sits again.)* It's a good thing they're asleep or you might have given them blood pressure. Fancy people writing stories like that! Disgusting, I call it. *(Settling down.)* Well, go on reading.
READER. That's the end.
ADVENTUROUS. The end! Honestly, you are the limit. I was just beginning to get interested. Do you mean to tell me it ends with those burning kisses on her frozen lips?
READER *(looking at book).* Yes—except that there's a row of dots across the page after that.
ADVENTUROUS *(knowingly).* Ah, I thought there would be.
 (HUNGRY ONE *throws an imaginary stone at the audience.)*
What are you doing?

HUNGRY (*throwing another*). Throwing stones in the sea.
ADVENTUROUS. I bet I can throw one further than you.
HUNGRY. I bet you can't.
ADVENTUROUS. All right then. (*Throws.*) Beat that then.
HUNGRY (*throwing*). There!
ADVENTUROUS (*getting up and selecting a better imaginary stone*). This will beat you anyway. (*Throws.*)
HUNGRY (*getting up and throwing*). How about *that* then?
    (*They go on throwing ad lib., with suitable comments—* "Mine went beyond the second wave . . .," "I nearly hit that seagull . . .," "Look, there's a bottle; let's try and break it . . ." *etc.*)
READER (*who has left book on rock, and is looking at the heap left by the others*). I say, it looks as though they've left some sandwiches for us. (*Lifts box and shows them.*)
HUNGRY (*taking box*). Oh good, I'm hungry.
ADVENTUROUS. They've left rather a lot, haven't they?
HUNGRY. No, we can soon get through these. The sea air always gives me an appetite.
READER. Let's take them with us and walk back the way we came.
HUNGRY. That's right, and we can eat them as we go. (*Biting a sandwich.*) Come on.
ADVENTUROUS (*as they go off down* L.). I wish I knew where the others had gone. (*Goes out.*)
READER. It doesn't matter; we shall see them at tea-time. (*Goes out.*)
HUNGRY. And that won't be long now, thank goodness. (*Goes out.*)
    (*Re-enter* MOTHER, R.)
MOTHER (*to the imaginary* GEORGIE). Seagulls eggs? I'll give you seagulls eggs, you little horror. Now go and play on the sand, and stay where I can see you. (*Sees sandwiches have gone.*) Oh glory, where have the sandwiches gone? Jack-er-leen! Come here. Have you been at them sandwiches? Tell Mummy the truth now. Open your mouth and let me look. Oh gracious, here come the others back.
    (*Re-enter all the others of the first party, up* L.)
INFORMATIVE. They weren't there. There's nobody in the next bay at all. They must have gone.
MOTHER. So have our sandwiches.
ALL. What?
MOTHER. I only left them for a moment to fetch young Georgie off the rocks, and when I came back, they'd disappeared.
    (ALL *search, making ad lib. comments—*" . . . they were just here . . .," "couldn't have walked away . . .," " . . . I don't trust those kids . . .," *etc.*)
INFORMATIVE. I say, you don't think—(*indicates* OLDEST RESIDENTS.)—?
YOUNG. What a lark! (*Going close to* OLDEST RESIDENT, R.) No, I don't think so.

CHEERY (*close to* SECOND OLDEST RESIDENT, L.). No, it couldn't have been them.
ANXIOUS (*up* C.). Could it have been smugglers? (ALL *stare.*) I mean—burglars—or—anyone?
INFORMATIVE. Well, of course it must have been someone. (*Spotting book on rock* L.) Hullo, what's this? A clue I think.
SECRETARY. Yes, yes, I know whose book that is.
INFORMATIVE. So do I. The others must have been here. But how could they get here without our meeting them?
MOTHER. Jacqueline, have you seen anybody come round here? . . . Three of them, eh? . . . Where did they come from? . . . Oh, round the bottom of the cliff, did they?
INFORMATIVE. Well, that solves the mystery.
READER (*off, up* L.). Oo—oo! (ALL *look up.*)
INFORMATIVE (*pointing up to top of cliff, off*). There they are. (*Calling.*) Did you take the sandwiches?
READER (*off*). Yes, thank you.
HUNGRY (*off*). And they were very nice too.
INFORMATIVE (*calling*). But we haven't had any yet!
  (ALL *make exclamations of surprise and alarm.*)
ADVENTUROUS (*off*). Come on up. The driver says if we go now, we shall have time to do some shopping before tea. He'll take us straight to Woolworths and Marks and Spencers.
INFORMATIVE. Come along then, we'd better go. Gather everything up.
ANXIOUS. Oh dear, this is not a very pleasant outing, is it? (*Goes out up* L.)
CHEERY. Cheer up, it might have been pouring with rain all day. (*Goes out.*)
GLOOMY. I wish it had. As it is, I've brought my umbrella for nothing. (*Goes out.*)
PRESIDENT (*to* SECRETARY). You'd better bring your shoes. (*Goes out.*)
SECRETARY (*picking up shoes*). Oh, someone has filled them with sand! (*Goes out.*)
MOTHER. Jackerleen, did you touch them shoes? I'll tan the hide off you. Yes I will—and you, Georgie. Get up that path the pair of you, or I'll give you both to a policeman. (*Goes out.*)
YOUNG (*picking up last bundle*). I think that's the lot. (*Goes out.*)
KNITTER. 397, 398, 399. Oh dear.
INFORMATIVE. What's the matter?
KNITTER. There should be 400. I must have dropped a stitch somewhere.
INFORMATIVE. Well, we can't go back and look for it now. Come along. (*They both go off.*)
SECOND OLDEST RESIDENT (*waking up after a few seconds, and leaning over.*) Eh?—er—was that you?
OLDEST RESIDENT (*stirring*). What's that?

Second Oldest Resident. Did you say something just now?
Oldest Resident. Did I? Oh yes, I was just going to say: What a lovely quiet spot this is.

Black-Out or Quick Curtain

PRODUCTION NOTES

Sea Side Trippers, like its predecessor *Spring Song Singers,* has been specially written for quick learning and easy staging, and requires few rehearsals.

Scenery is quite unnecessary, and a few large notices will be found very effective: for example, on the back wall of the stage could be a placard printed—"THE CLIFFS," or if you prefer it—"DO NOT DAMAGE THESE CLIFFS. PENALTY £5", etc. The rocks, if they are suitably draped, should be fairly obvious; but just to make quite sure, you could erect a notice board on top, stating—"IT IS DANGEROUS TO DIVE OFF THESE ROCKS," or something similar.

Costumes can vary from the sublime to the ridiculous: The YOUNG ONE will probably favour something rather smart in beach-wear, while the GLOOMY ONE will almost certainly wear a winter coat. The rest can be as colourful or atrocious as they like.

THE OLDEST RESIDENTS must keep quite still during all the time that the other characters are on the stage, but if they are turned well away, and sufficiently concealed from the audience, there is no reason why one or both of them should not have books, and act as prompters. The INFORMATIVE ONE can also conceal a copy of the script inside the guide book, if desired. Nobody else has more than twelve lines to learn, except the MOTHER, and she has only sixteen.

In the stage directions, everybody's entrance and exit takes place on the Left, except for the few minutes that the MOTHER disappears on the Right. If your stage has more room in the wings on the other side, then merely change everything round the other way, and make your main entrance up R. It would be also quite effective to let the ADVENTUROUS, HUNGRY and READER enter from *outside* the proscenium arch and climb up on to the stage, as if they had been wading through the water.

Sea Side Trippers can be performed with a mixed cast, or with a cast of all the same sex. What fun it would be to put it on with an entirely male cast!

R.T.

Snow White Special

A Dwarf Panto of a Minidrama

Richard Tydeman

A Samuel French Acting Edition

FOUNDED 1830

SAMUELFRENCH-LONDON.CO.UK
SAMUELFRENCH.COM

CHARACTERS
(in the order of their appearance)

THE COMPERE, *who has a book*
GUSTAV, *the Royal Wizard's Assistant*
JAYBEE, *the Royal Wizard himself*
SNOW WHITE, *a Very Special Laundry-Maid*
QUEEN ERMYNTRUDE, *a Wicked Aunt*
TWO ATTENDANTS, *male or female*
THE SEVEN DWARFS,
    Monday, Tuesday, Wednesday, Thursday,
    Friday, Saturday and Sunday

SCENES: The Magic Mirror Room at the Palace, and the Dwarfs' Cottage.

SNOW WHITE SPECIAL

The COMPERE, *carrying a copy of the script, appears before the curtain.*

COMPERE. Kind friends, I pray you, give me time
To introduce our Pantomime.
It's very short—and what is worse—
It's written in atrocious verse.
(I hope the acting's not the same,
Or else you'll wish you never came!)
You've read, of course, in story books,
About the girl whose beauteous looks
And Persil-washed complexion bright
Have earned for her the name "Snow White."
Those story books you must not heed,
They are not truthful; no indeed,
Such tales no thinking person swallows!
The *real* story is as follows:—
Act One. A palace. Long ago.
The curtain rises now, to show

(Curtain rises. GUSTAV *is busy with something that looks like a primitive wireless set with many loose wires, behind a large gauze-covered picture frame—the "magic mirror.")*

Gustav, the Royal Wizard's mate.

GUSTAV. Cor flip, I 'ope the boss ain't late;
I don't know 'ow to work the doin's.

(There is a flash or bang from GUSTAV'S *apparatus.)*

COMPERE. This lad will have the place in ruins!
What is this strange contraption, sirrah?

GUSTAV. It's s'posed to be a magic mirror.

COMPERE. Ah yes. Good friends, you've heard about
This magic glass, I have no doubt.
The Queen consults it every day,
And presently you'll hear her say:—
"Mirror, mirror, on the wall,
Who is the fairest one of all?"
To which replies the looking-glass:—
"Your Majesty doth all surpass."
This interesting little custom
We'll now observe.

(A bigger flash or bang from the apparatus.)

GUSTAV. Oh 'eck, I've bust 'em!

COMPERE. What *are* you doing?

GUSTAV. I dunno,
I just can't get the thing to go.

SNOW WHITE SPECIAL

COMPERE. But here comes real cause for worry—
Jaybee the Wizard, in a hurry.
(Enter JAYBEE, *the Royal Wizard.)*
JAYBEE. Come, switch on quick, and help me in it.
We'll have the Queen here any minute.
(He starts to get behind the "mirror.")
COMPERE. Good sir, your bold assistant here
Has got into a mess, I fear.
JAYBEE. Oh no! I told him how to work it.
GUSTAV. Five valves gone west on one short circuit.
JAYBEE. You surely can't have broken five!
(He reaches into the apparatus.)
GUSTAV. Look out, I think that wire's alive.
*(*JAYBEE *jumps back and hops about sucking fingers.)*
JAYBEE. Of all the stupid blundering dolts,
You've filled my fingers full of volts!
(Exit JAYBEE, R.*)*
COMPERE. While Jaybee goes to seek first-aid,
In comes Snow White, the laundry maid.
(Enter SNOW WHITE, R.*)*
Our Gustav rises to his feet;
He feels his heart begin to beat.
(And we can hear his heart beating; drum in the wings.)
SNOW WHITE. Whatever's bitten poor Jaybee?
GUSTAV. He isn't very pleased with me.
COMPERE. And that is quite—I sadly fear—
The understatement of the year.
The maid advances to the table
Where Gustav shows the offending cable.
Her nimble fingers deftly fix
The wires inside the box of tricks;
And now she straightens up to say:—
SNOW WHITE. I think you'll find that's quite O.K.
COMPERE. As Gustav gazes at her proudly.
His heart is beating very loudly.
(And so is the drum in the wings.)
And bowing in a manner dashing,
He says:—
GUSTAV. Cor flip, I think you're smashing!
COMPERE. A compliment, I would have said,
That might be misinterpreted.
But Gustav's heart has ceased to beat,
For he has heard the sound of feet
Approaching with a regal tread.
GUSTAV. The Queen!
SNOW WHITE. All right, don't lose your head.
COMPERE. So saying, this resourceful dame
Shoves Gustav in the picture-frame,

	And giving him a loving look
	She starts to check the laundry-book.

(SNOW WHITE *is checking laundry down* L. GUSTAV, C., *is behind the "magic mirror". Enter,* R., *two* ATTENDANTS *walking backwards in front of the* QUEEN.)

1ST ATTEND.	Make way, make way, and bow the knee
	Before Her Gracious Majesty,
2ND ATTEND.	Queen Ermyntrude, the Queen of Beauty.
QUEEN.	I thank you both; you've done your duty.
1ST ATTEND.	Be silent all before the Queen.
QUEEN.	All right.
2ND ATTEND.	And let no frowns be seen.
1ST ATTEND.	Her Majesty with joy shall fill you.
QUEEN.	All right.
2ND ATTEND.	Make way—
QUEEN.	Oh shut up, will you!
COMPERE.	The questioning's about to start.
	(Let's hope that Gustav's learnt his part!)
	With carriage proud, and step serene,
	Towards the mirror moves the Queen.
QUEEN.	Mirror, mirror on the wall,
	Who is the fairest one of all?
COMPERE.	Instead of Jaybee's prompt reply,
	The mirror seems to give a sigh
	As Gustav bites his bottom lip
	And softly murmers:—
GUSTAV.	Ooh, cor flip.
COMPERE.	Impatiently the Queen once more
	Repeats the question as before.
QUEEN.	Mirror, mirror on the wall,
	Who is the fairest one of all?
SNOW WHITE	(*prompting in a whisper*).
	Your Majesty doth all surpass.
GUSTAV.	Your Majesty's as bold as brass.
SNOW WHITE	(*still whispering*).
	No, no, I never told you that!
GUSTAV.	I mean you're very old and fat.
QUEEN	(*angrily*). What's this?
SNOW WHITE	(*in an anxious whisper*). Do get the answer right!
GUSTAV.	I mean the fairest one's Snow White.
QUEEN.	So ho! My magic mirror rare,
	You think my laundry-maid is fair?
	This day for her shall be the last.
	Seize yonder maid and hold her fast.
	(*The* ATTENDANTS *seize* SNOW WHITE.)
	In darkest forest set her free,
	About the time the lions have tea.
	I think we'll find that by tonight

	Only her bones will still be white!
	(Exit QUEEN R. *with a horrible laugh.)*
COMPERE.	Exit the Queen, with horrid laughter.
	Snow White is quickly hustled after.
	(ATTENDANTS *take* SNOW WHITE *off* R.)
	As Gustav cries in sore distress:—
GUSTAV.	Cor Lumme, what a flipping mess!
	(The curtain falls, leaving the COMPERE *outside.)*
COMPERE.	Far off they take the hapless maid,
	And dump her in a forest glade
	Where hungry creatures have their lairs,
	And leave her to the lions and bears.
	But near that spot, among the trees
	A funny little house she sees,
	With seven chimneys in a row,
	And seven little windows low,
	And seven little rooms inside;
	For there the Seven Dwarfs reside.
	And here they are, their day's work done,
	Arriving home at set of sun.
	(They're really little tiny men,
	The tallest only two foot ten;
	But so as not to hurt your eyes,
	We've magnified them double size.)

(The curtain rises to show interior of Dwarfs' Cottage. A table; a bench or boxes to sit on; an imitation T.V. set down L. *March. Enter the* SEVEN DWARFS—*but see Production Notes for instructions if less than seven available.)*

	Good evening to you, little elves;
	Perhaps you'll introduce yourselves
MONDAY.	Seven little Dwarfs are we.
TUESDAY.	Nicer Dwarfs you'll never see.
WEDNESDAY.	Our names are:—Wednesday,
TUESDAY.	Tuesday,
MONDAY.	Monday,
THURSDAY.	Thursday,
FRIDAY.	Friday,
SATURDAY.	Saturday,
SUNDAY.	Sunday.
COMPERE.	Delightful names; they suit you well;
	But how you got them, who can tell?
WEDNESDAY.	The reason's not so hard to seek:
	You see, we're just a little weak.
THURSDAY.	The Magistrate—to coin a phrase—
	Told Dad he'd give him seven days.
FRIDAY.	Dad says our names remind him still
	Of holidays in Pentonville.
SATURDAY.	So now our story we've repeated.

SNOW WHITE SPECIAL

COMPERE. I thank you, Dwarfs. Do please be seated.
(*Opportunity here for funny business. E.g.—They all sit, but* MONDAY *sits on the second seat instead of the first, and therefore* SUNDAY *has no seat and falls on floor. He gets up and pushes* SATURDAY, *who pushes* FRIDAY, *etc. Eventually* MONDAY *moves on to first seat and all move up one. Meantime,* SUNDAY *moves round to other end of line, just as they have all moved along. He pushes* MONDAY, *etc., and all move down again. Meanwhile,* SUNDAY *goes back to the other end just as they have all moved along. He scratches his head, gives* SATURDAY *a big push; all move along, and* SUNDAY *sits.*)
Ah good. That's better. Now let's hear
How things are going.
MONDAY. Bad, I fear.
TUESDAY. Our tyres are flat; our bikes have rusted;
WEDNESDAY. The lights have fused; the T.V's busted;
THURSDAY. The copper kettle's sprung a leak;
FRIDAY. The mangle's got an awful squeak;
SATURDAY. The paper off the walls is peeling,
SUNDAY. There's death watch beetle in the ceiling.
MONDAY. The ugly truth we'll have to face:
We need a man about the place.
(*All shake their heads sadly.*)
TUESDAY. Well, now we've said our little piece,
It's time to go and feed the geese.
THURSDAY. And wrap some leather round our legs.
FRIDAY. And search the nettle patch for eggs.
SATURDAY. Each take a stick, and if attacked
You all know how you ought to act.
(*They rise and arm themselves with sticks.*)
COMPERE. So now the Dwarfs their weapons take.
It seems a lot of fuss to make;
It really looks a bit absurd
To go out armed against a bird.
SUNDAY. Now look here mate, before you chide us,
Don't forget you've magnified us.
If you could come outside, you'd see
The gander's twice as big as me.
COMPERE. Of course, I'd quite forgotten that.
Well, do be careful what you're at.
(*Exit* DWARFS, R.)
So off they go with courage rash,
To give the geese their daily mash.
But hardly have they left before
A knock sounds at the other door,
And seeking shelter for the night
Appears our heroine, Snow White.
(*Enter* SNOW WHITE, L.)

SNOW WHITE SPECIAL

SNOW WHITE.   She scarcely can believe her eyes,
And looks around in great surprise.
This place is in a shocking state.
I'll have to try and put it straight.
(During the next speech, SNOW WHITE moves quickly about the stage cleaning and repairing imaginary articles.)
COMPERE.   Then, in a most efficient manner
She fetches out her pocket spanner,
Pliers, screw-driver, oilcan,
To make the place look spick and span.
In less time than it takes to tell,
The T.V. set is working well;
The mangle's had a lovely oiling;
The mended copper kettle's boiling;
The house is clean from floor to thatch;
The death watch beetle's met his match;
While seven bikes, with tyres inflated,
Stand gleaming as if silver-plated.
(I trust that your imagination
Can cope with such a situation?)
(Exit SNOW WHITE L.)
Exhausted now, the maiden goes
Upstairs to seek well-earned repose
And rest her weary feet and legs.
Re-enter Dwarfs, with goose's eggs.
(Re-enter DWARFS R. carrying enormous eggs. They gaze about.)
They gaze around in consternation
At such a wondrous transformation,
And blink at all the shining metal
On mangle, bikes and copper kettle.
MONDAY.   Whoever could have been in here?
TUESDAY.   There's more than one; that's very clear.
WEDNESDAY.   Perhaps they sent the army?
THURSDAY.   Yes,
Or else the W.V.S.
FRIDAY.   No mortals work at such a pace;
They must have come from Outer Space.
SATURDAY.   The house has never looked so clean;
SUNDAY.   And "Six-Five Special's" on the screen!
(All crowd round T.V. set as SUNDAY turns volume up and music is heard. Opportunity for dance, skiffle group, etc.)
COMPERE.   Awakened by the noisy din,
Snow White now quickly hurries in.
(Enter SNOW WHITE L. They switch off T.V. and stare.)
SNOW WHITE.   Now then, you naughty little boys,
Stop making all that dreadful noise.
COMPERE.   At first this makes the Dwarfs defiant:

TUESDAY.	We're not afraid of you, you giant!
	(But they all try to hide behind each other.)
COMPERE.	Then, noticing her box of tools,
	The leader cries:
MONDAY.	What silly fools
	We are to get in such a panic;
	This must be our unknown mechanic!
COMPERE.	Snow White admits that this is true.
SNOW WHITE.	I'd like to stay and work for you.
COMPERE.	The Dwarfs all try to make amends,
	And soon they are the best of friends,
	They turn the music on once more,
	And all together take the floor.

(SUNDAY turns music on again and all dance, etc. Curtain slowly falls, leaving COMPERE outside. Music dies away.)

    So thus Snow White the office took
Of foster-mother, housewife, cook,
Of electrician, engineer—
And time ran on for half a year.
Meanwhile within the palace grey,
Poor Gustav nearly pined away.
But now the Queen begins to hear
Reports that fill her heart with fear:
Within the forest, so 'tis said,
There dwells a maid who's far from dead,
And every day her beauty grows.
The jealous Queen with anger glows;
Proceeding to disguise herself,
She takes an apple from the shelf,
Scoops out the fruit and puts inside
Potassium of cyanide!
So, as the curtain once more rises,
Prepare yourselves for more surprises.

(Curtain rises. SNOW WHITE is sitting in a chair, C., reading to the DWARFS who are sitting on the floor.)

SNOW WHITE.	So Sleeping Beauty came to life
	And soon became the Prince's wife.
	The palace rang with joy and laughter,
	And all lived happy ever after.

(She closes the book.)

TUESDAY.	Oh, don't stop yet! We'll all be good.
WEDNESDAY.	Please read about Red Riding Hood.
THURSDAY.	Or Goldilocks who met the bears.
SNOW WHITE.	No no, it's time to go upstairs.

    (DWARFS all sigh, rise, and say goodnight.)
    Good night then, Wednesday, Tuesday, Monday,
    Thursday, Friday, Saturday, Sunday.

SNOW WHITE SPECIAL

                (DWARFS *exit up* L.)
COMPERE. So off they go. And Snow White, yawning,
            Goes off as well, to sleep till morning.
     (SNOW WHITE *yawns and exits up* L. *Enter* R. *the* QUEEN,
     in cloak and hood, carrying an apple.)
            But who is this, so darkly gliding,
            Beneath her cloak an apple hiding?
            Yes, yes, I'm sure you've recognised
            The bad Queen Ermyntrude, disguised.
QUEEN. I say Snow White shall die! So be it.
            I'll leave this apple where she'll see it.
            One bite of this, however small,
            And *I'll* be fairest one of all.
     (*She leaves apple on chair and exits with low chuckle.*)
COMPERE. But little has the Queen divined
            That someone else is close behind,
            And hardly has she left the place,
            When round the corner comes the face
            Of faithful Gustav, all suspicious,
              (*Enter* GUSTAV, R., *cautiously.*)
            He sees the apple so delicious;
            He lifts the poison to his nose,
            Inhales the fumes, and down he goes!
     (GUSTAV *smells apple, and making a lot of noise, falls
unconscious in the chair, with apple still held to nose.*)
            The noise he makes is so distressing
            That down the stairs the Dwarfs come pressing.
     (*Re-enter* DWARFS. GUSTAV *is now stiff and silent.*)
            They gaze in horror at the sight,
            And one runs off to fetch Snow White.
              (*Exit* SUNDAY.)
MONDAY. Another giant! Dead, I fear.
            I wish he hadn't died in here.
TUESDAY. He's such a size! We'll never lift him.
WEDNESDAY. We'll have to cut him up to shift him.
THURSDAY. I'll get a knife. (*Exit.*)
FRIDAY.   I'll get a spade.
SATURDAY. I'll go and get a coffin made.
TUESDAY. I wonder if he's Church or Chapel?
            (*Re-enter* SNOW WHITE *and* SUNDAY.)
COMPERE. But Snow White enters, takes the apple,
            Throws it away, and with a sigh
            Our Gustav opens half an eye.
            Then opens both.
THURSDAY (*re-entering*). Now here's a knife.
WEDNESDAY. Too late; I think he's come to life.
SNOW WHITE. Tell them you've come to life, dear Gustav.
GUSTAV. Cor flip, well yes, I s'pose I must have.

COMPERE.	With that, he takes his lady's hand.
	The tactful Dwarfs all understand.

(*The* DWARFS *turn away with their hands clasped behind them, whistling.*)

When through the window, suddenly
Appears the Wizard, old Jaybee.
(*Enter* JAYBEE, *preferably through the audience.*)
He carries in his hand two scrolls
Which now he carefully unrolls.

JAYBEE.	This parchment proves,
COMPERE.	He says,
JAYBEE.	that you,

Gustav, are King of Timbuctoo!
While Snow White here is nothing less
Than Lady Blanche, the Crown Princess.
(*Re-enter* QUEEN. *She kneels and offers* SNOW WHITE *a bright yellow cardboard crown.*)

QUEEN. My child, forgive your wicked aunt.
I tried to kill you, but I can't.
So take my crown—I've had it sprayed,
And I will be your laundry-maid.
(*Tableau. The two* ATTENDANTS *enter with a crown for* GUSTAV, *or orb and sceptre, etc.*)

COMPERE. Well, all this is, as you can see,
Extremely satisfactory.
Snow White and Gustav now can wed,
And occupy the throne instead.
So that's the *real* tale, my friends,
And there, I fear, our story ends.

MONDAY. I say, I hate to make a fuss,
But haven't you forgotten us?

COMPERE. Ah yes, the Dwarfs; I beg your pardon.
In every small suburban garden
Your figures shall for ever be
Found standing round the rockery.
So finishes my humble task;
To give the final word I'll ask.
King Gustav and Her Ladyship.

SNOW WHITE. I'll say Good night.

GUSTAV. I'll say—(*He is tongue-tied*)—Cor flip!

CURTAIN.

(*Production notes at end of play.*)

SNOW WHITE SPECIAL

PRODUCTION NOTES

Those who have already produced other Minidramas will hardly need Production Notes for this one. Briefly, everything has been kept to a minimum, of words to learn, scenery and props., costume-making, and stage directions. The enterprising producer is left a very free hand! Play at a good pace, with everyone saying the exact words allotted to them, neither more nor less, to bring out the full "atrocity" of the verse.

The Magic Mirror merely needs a large picture frame covered with gauze, set at an angle so that the audience can see GUSTAV behind it, but the QUEEN cannot. The T.V. set in the Dwarfs' Cottage can be a large cardboard box, so that the "screen" is turned away from the audience.

Costumes can be "fairy story" type, concocted from the wardrobe and the rag-bag. The DWARFS can be as big as you like, and the bigger they are the funnier it will be. Dress them as much alike as possible, preferably like those little terra-cotta rockery ornaments, with pointed red hats and Wellington boots.

If your company cannot manage as many as Seven Dwarfs, you can play the piece with only Four—Monday, Wednesday, Friday and Sunday, sharing the others' lines among them. In this case, put large labels on them, saying "1," "3," "5" and "7," and insert the following lines after "Seven Little Dwarfs are we: Nicer Dwarfs you'll never see.":—

COMPERE. Did you say Seven? Are you sure?
To me it only looks like four.
MONDAY. We had to come without our mates;
No Parking here on Even Dates.

This Minidrama is designed for a mixed cast, but it can just as easily be played by all men or all women if preferred.—R.T.

Albert Laddin

A Storm in a China Tea-Cup

Richard Tydeman

A SAMUEL FRENCH ACTING EDITION

SAMUELFRENCH-LONDON.CO.UK
SAMUELFRENCH.COM

Another Panto-Minidrama to follow *Red Hot Cinders, Forty Winks Beauty, Ali's Barbara* and *Snow White Special*. Ten or more characters of either sex. Simple to dress and stage; little to learn; easy to rehearse.

CHARACTERS

in order of appearance

THE GENIE, *who acts as narrator*
ALBERT ("AL") LADDIN, *a promising youth*
ABANAZAR, *his wizard wicked uncle*
WIDOW TWANKY, *Al's mother*
THE EMPRESS OF CHINA
THE PRINCESS, *her daughter*
DAY-GLOW ⎫
KIS-MEE   ⎬ *ladies-in-waiting*
MEE-TOO   ⎪
OO-MUM   ⎭

The scene varies, at a wave of the Genie's hand, from Albert's house to the Empress's Boudoir, the Cavern of the Wonderful Lamp, and Albert's Palace.

ALBERT LADDIN

When the curtain rises, the GENIE *is seen in the* C. *of the stage. He appears to be enormous, for he is actually standing on a chair with outstretched arms, and is clothed with flowing garments and draperies that reach the floor. He also wears a coloured turban and a fantastic make-up.*

GENIE. Frail mortals attend me, and listen and hear;
Oh shrink not in terror, there's nothing to fear.
'tis true I'm enormous, but all of my figure
Is spirit, not flesh, so it makes me look bigger.
I can flutter through walls that would baffle Houdini,
For I am the true and original Genie.
And if anyone mentions my "light brown hair"—
Too late! I've heard it before. So *there!* (*Sticking tongue out.*)
But to prove that I'm not an unsociable devil
I'll bring myself down to a human-size level.
  (*And he steps down from the chair, gathering up his draperies.* ALBERT, *who has been standing behind the* GENIE *all this time concealed from view, now sits in the chair.*)
I think that's a style that I don't look too bad in.
And now for the story of young Albert Laddin.
  (*He moves to the side of stage, produces a copy of the script, and acts as narrator, compère and prompter.* ALBERT *is now revealed.*)
There he sits—Mr. Laddin, the pantomime's pal.

ALBERT. My full name is Albert, but please call me Al.

GENIE. Our story will certainly have to begin
With the day Abanazar, Al's uncle, blew in.
  (*Enter* UNCLE ABANAZAR, *looking particularly wicked.* ALBERT *rises and greets him silently.*)
Black sheep of the clan is this bad Uncle Abe.

UNCLE. My dear sir, I'm as pure as a newly-born babe. (*He leers at the audience and chuckles wickedly.*)

GENIE. At that moment from outside the door Albert hears
A—

TWANKY (*off*). Yoo-hoo!

GENIE.   And soon in the doorway appears
His mother, a laundress of vest, shirt and hanky,

Who's known to her friends as the gay Widow Twanky.

(*Enter* WIDOW TWANKY, *a typical pantomime dame, wearing a funny hat with a tall nodding flower sticking out of the top. She ignores all the people on the stage, comes* D.C. *and addresses the audience—in prose!*)

TWANKY. 'Ullo, 'ullo, 'ullo. 'ow are you, eh? All 'appy and smiling? That's right. (*Waving to someone on the left of the fifth row.*) 'ullo Charlie, 'ow's Gladys? Give 'er my love. (*Turning to someone on* R. *of same row.*) What's the matter with you, dear? Too tight are they? Well, take 'em off, we don't mind; we're broad-minded. (*With mock horror.*) Oh no, madam, I didn't mean you; I was talking about that gentleman's boots. (C. *again.*) 'ere, I must tell you this; d'you know, as I was coming to the theatre tonight—

(ALBERT *and* UNCLE *have been standing impatiently with hands on hips. The* GENIE, *exasperated, now interrupts.*)

GENIE. My dear madam, this piece has been written in rhyme.
You're supposed to speak only in verse all the time.

TWANKY. Oh, I can't be bothered to do that, ducky. I never agreed with all this verse rubbish in the first place, and now I'm up 'ere I'm going to say just what I like and 'ow I like. (*Pulls hat firmly down on head and addresses someone in front row.*) Oh, you're here tonight, are you? Well, watch your step. I saw your old woman (*or* "*old man*") looking for you outside. I bet she (*Or* "*he*".) doesn't know who you're with! Oh, you naughty old thing you! Now I was telling you—as I was coming to the theatre tonight—

ALBERT (*stepping forward and speaking loudly*).
Dear mother, my uncle invites me to go
To look for some treasure. Please may I?

TWANKY. No, no!
There, you've got me doing it now. Well, I refuse to speak in rhyme, so I'll say "Yes, yes" instead. (*To* GENIE.) That'll fox you, won't it? Run along then, Al, and don't be late for supper. And talking about being late, I nearly forgot: I'm supposed to be ironing the Empress's handkerchief. She's only got one, so I mustn't keep her waiting. See you later. Toodle-oo.

(*With a wave at the audience she dances off singing,* "My old man said, 'Foller the van . . .' " *etc.*)

GENIE. We apologize very profoundly indeed
For this break in transmission. And now we'll proceed.

UNCLE. Come Al, my dear fellow, a journey let's take,
And without any effort your fortune I'll make.
        (To audience, with a leer.)
At least, to be perfectly true to the letter,
He's going to make mine, which is very much better.
ALBERT. Dear Uncle, before I fulfil my ambition,
Please tell me if you are indeed a magician?
UNCLE. Most certainly, lad, and I'll prove it. Watch me;
Here's a trick you can try on your friends after tea.
        (And he performs a simple but effective conjuring trick.)
Away then we fly to the cave and the treasure,
And live ever after in riches and pleasure.
        (Exeunt UNCLE and ALBERT.)
GENIE. Let the curtain be drawn *(Curtain moves slowly.)*
        —oh, but very much quicker!
When Genies are working you have to look slicker.
        (Curtain falls rapidly, leaving GENIE outside.)
That's better. Now, mortals, hold tight to your chair,
For I'm going to take you at speed through the air,
        (Raises hand; whistling noise off; lowers hand.)
And land you, before you can say "Mickey Finn",
In the Emperor's palace in ancient Pekin,
        (The GENIE gestures to the curtain, which rises, disclosing the EMPEROR'S palace. The EMPRESS is sitting, surrounded by four or more Ladies-in-Waiting named DAY-GLOW, KIS-MEE, MEE-TOO, OO-MUM, etc. The PRINCESS is also present.)
Where we find in a boudoir, all gaily debating,
The Empress, her daughter, and ladies-in-waiting.
The Princess's name is: (for so I've been taught)
"Shooting-Star-Shining-Brightly"—or "Shoo-shine" for short.
EMPRESS. Now, Shoo-shine my daughter, I pray you come hither,
And practise your singing while I play the zither.
        (The EMPRESS strums on an unidentified and badly-tuned string instrument while SHOO-SHINE warbles a very discordant "eastern" tune. The LADIES very gracefully put their fingers into their ears.)
GENIE. I hasten to tell you, dear mortals, that that's
Genu-*ine* Chinese music, and not squalling cats!
DAY-GLOW *(at window)*. Your Highness—

EMPRESS (*turning impatiently*). Well, really!
DAY-GLOW. Your pardon, great Queen,
But a young man of elegant beauty I've seen.
GENIE. At once there's a scramble from cushion and chair
To the window, as each eager lady asks:
ALL (*rushing to window*). Where?
SHOO-SHINE. 'tis he! 'tis young Albert, the laundress's boy!
GENIE. So saying, the Princess falls swooning with joy.
(*And the* LADIES *catch her and lay her down*.)
EMPRESS. Did you hear her say "Albert"? Extraordinary name.
KIS-MEE. Your Majesty, I was just thinking the same.
MEE-TOO. Surely Albert was eaten by lions at a zoo?
OO-MUM. No, I think it's a watch-chain—a heavy one, too.
EMPRESS. An Albert? No, no, you're both wrong, I'm afraid;
It's a Hall where the Promenade Concerts are played.
GENIE. By this time the Princess begins to awaken.
(SHOO-SHINE *sits up*.)
EMPRESS. My daughter, I very much hope I'm mistaken,
But are you attracted by that lowly youth?
GENIE. Poor Shoo-Shine is torn between trouble and truth.
She is saved by a knock at the Empress's door,
And in comes a lady you've all met before.
(*Enter* WIDOW TWANKY.)
TWANKY. Good afternoon, your 'ighness, I've brought back your 'andkerchief nicely washed in that 'igh quality Chinese detergent—"Pong", and carefully ironed with me own fair 'ands. There you are, ma'am. That'll be seven and a tanner, but you can pay me next week. (D.S., *to audience*.) 'ere, 'ave you 'eard the story about the Chinese laundryman who emptied a packet of cornflakes into his washing machine instead of soapflakes? The machine got all Kellogged up! Get it? Clogged—Kellogged—cornflakes—no? (GENIE *coughs loudly*.) Oh dear, there's old Thunderguts complaining again. See you later.
(*Exit singing, as before*.)
GENIE. So now we go on.
EMPRESS. No, indeed sir, we don't.
We will *not* be insulted like that.
LADIES. No, we won't.
GENIE. Dear ladies, I pray you—

EMPRESS. Let's leave him alone;
He can just play the rest of this scene on his own.
           (*They start to go.*)
GENIE. But what shall I do, ma'am?
EMPRESS.   I really can't tell.
I forget the Chinese for "a soldier's farewell".
           (*Exit.*)
GENIE. Close the scene! Drop the curtain! (*Curtain falls.*)
                         Dear mortals, with shame
I ask you to witness that I'm not to blame.
But of all the afflictions with which men are cursed,
Surely jealous and jabbering women are worst.
So, back to the men, Abe and Al, who have passed
The palace and come to that cavern at last
Where the treasure is guarded from thieves and from damp
By the magical power of a Wonderful Lamp.
           (ALBERT *and* UNCLE *appear, preferably up the middle of the hall.*
       ALBERT *is trying over the trick that* UNCLE *showed him earlier.*)
UNCLE. That's right, my dear fellow, you've got it off pat;
And here is another one, better than that.
           (*And having mounted the stage, in front of the curtain,* UNCLE
       performs another conjuring trick. As he finishes, the GENIE *gestures to
       the curtain, which rises, disclosing the Cavern.* C. *is a box marked
       "Treasure", and standing on it is a dirty and disreputable-looking lamp.
       On one side is the "Entrance". See Production Notes.*)
But come this way, laddie, and now you can see
Why your help is so very essential to me;
The door of this cave is so narrow that I
Could never get through it, however I try.
           (ALBERT *climbs through the "Entrance".*)
ALBERT. Don't worry, dear Uncle, it's easy. I'm through.
Now tell me just what you would like me to do.
UNCLE. The treasure, my boy, you can keep for yourself.
Just bring me the lamp which you'll find on a shelf.
ALBERT. This dirty old lamp?
UNCLE (*looking round anxiously*). That's the one, boy. Make haste.
ALBERT. Well, I can't say I think very much of your taste.
Help me out.
           (*But* UNCLE *is still anxiously looking the other way.*)

GENIE. But instead of providing assistance,
Abe suddenly vanishes into the distance. (*Exit* UNCLE.)
A passing policeman had given him cause
To move on. Uncle Abe is no friend of the Law's.
So Albert is left in the cave ruminating:
ALBERT. I might as well clean up this lamp while I'm waiting.
GENIE. And setting to work with the sleeve of his shirt,
He starts to remove all the layers of dirt.
But before he can get even half of it clean,
An enormous great Genie appears on the scene.
(*Nothing happens.*)
I repeat, an enormous great Genie—oh dear
I'd forgotten, that's me. (*Stepping forward.*)
Mighty Prince, I appear.
ALBERT. Who are you?
GENIE. O great master, I come to your call;
I'm the Slave of the Lamp. Your commands great and small
I obey without question; so say what you're lacking,
And swift as greased lightning I'll go and get cracking.
ALBERT. A Genie? I'm dreaming! Go, fetch me, I pray,
An apple.
GENIE. Great master, I hear and obey. (*Hands him an apple.*)
ALBERT. It works! Now, good Genie, please could you transport a
Young lady named Shoo-Shine, the Emperor's daughter?
GENIE. No trouble at all, sir, so swift is my path.
(*Waves hand. Enter* SHOO-SHINE *wrapped in a bath-towel; she screams and exit.*)
I regret, the young lady was taking a bath.
But come my young friend, let me build you a place
That will even put smiles on the Empress's face;
Choose a suitable site in a first class position.
(We Genies don't bother with Planning Permission.)
ALBERT. Park Lane? (*Or some equally high-class locality elsewhere.*)
GENIE. By all means. Draw the curtain straightway,
(*Curtain falls leaving* ALBERT *outside with* GENIE.)
While a palace we build without further delay.
(*Waving hands.*)
Southern aspect, five storeys—with lift to all floors;
Purple paint with pink edges to windows and doors;

Forty bedrooms with H. and C. water laid on:
Eight recep., bath and kitchen, and every mod. con.
ALBERT. But that will take ages!
GENIE (*pointing to curtain*). Look out in the street—
I think you will find it already complete.
ALBERT. How on earth—? (*He is peeping behind the curtain.*)
GENIE. My dear fellow, don't ask how or why.
With Genies the Union rules don't apply.
Here's the key to the door. Go inside and inspect it;
If anything's wrong we can quickly correct it.
    (ALBERT *disappears behind the curtain.*)
And now, gentle mortals, imagine I pray
That some three months have passed, and we come to the day
Of Al's wedding to Shoo-Shine. For Al, you must know,
Is the wealthiest man from Shanghai to Soho;
And even an Emperor can't be so rash
As to turn down a son-in-law rolling in cash.
Behold then the feast, joy and happiness reigning—
Till the Bride and her mother begin entertaining.
    (*Curtain rises.* EMPRESS *with zither;* SHOO-SHINE *singing.* LADIES *with fingers in ears.* ALBERT *listening with an excruciating expression. As they finish,* ALBERT *applauds;* LADIES *quickly join in applause.*)
EMPRESS. And now we will render—
ALBERT (*quickly*). Dear Mother-in-law,
I fear you'll be tired if you play any more.
EMPRESS. Oh, nonsense.
DAY-GLOW. Your Highness, the Emperor said
We were not to be late; and it's past time for bed.
KIS-MEE. This music is quite the best part of the marriage,
But we mustn't be greedy—I'll order the carriage. (*Exit.*)
MEE-TOO (*to* SHOO-SHINE). We wish you all happiness, joy and good cheer.
OO-MUM. And may all your troubles be—
MEE-TOO. Come along, dear.
    (*Exeunt* LADIES. *The* EMPRESS *takes* SHOO-SHINE *aside.*)
EMPRESS. One word of advice: always keep the house clean.
Don't harbour old rubbish. (*Indicating the Lamp which is standing on a table.*) You know what I mean.

ALBERT. I'll just see you out.
EMPRESS. Please don't bother to come.
ALBERT. Oh, I'd like to.
EMPRESS. Good night, Shoo-Shine, dear.
SHOO-SHINE. Good night, Mum.
(*Exit* EMPRESS *and* ALBERT.)
GENIE. If you're squeamish, dear mortals, your eyes quickly veil,
For now comes the sorriest part of our tale.
Abanazar the wizard, Al's wicked old nunk,
Makes his entrance disguised as a dealer in junk.
(*Enter* UNCLE *disguised.*)
UNCLE. Any brass, any silver, old iron or gold?
GENIE. And Shoo-Shine, remembering what she's been told
Says:
SHOO-SHINE. Our gold and our silver's in vaults at the Banks;
But here's one piece of brass you can have.
UNCLE. Many thanks.
GENIE. From the table she reaches the Wonderful Lamp,
And delivers it up to that plausible scamp,
Who rubs it. Great Master, what would you with me?
UNCLE. Move us and this palace to Southend-on-Sea.
(*Or anywhere-else-on-sea.* GENIE *waves hand; there is a blackout, a whistling noise, and the lights go on again.* UNCLE, SHOO-SHINE *and the furniture have vanished.*)
GENIE. I hate to obey the commands of that knave;
But I dare not refuse, being only a Slave.
Now Al and the ladies, alarmed at the clatter,
Return in great haste to see what is the matter.
(*Re-enter* ALBERT, EMPRESS *and* LADIES.)
EMPRESS. Where's my daughter?
DAY-GLOW. Where's Shoo-Shine?
KIS-MEE. Al, where is your spouse?
MEE-TOO. Where's the step?
OO-MUM. Where's the door?
ALBERT. Where's the whole blooming house?
GENIE. Alas, sir, your uncle, that wicked old sharper,
Has taken the Lamp and effected a scapa.
ALBERT. Good Genie, I beg you to lend us your aid!
GENIE. I would if I could, but I can't, I'm afraid.

EMPRESS. Oh, what shall we do then?
GENIE.   Dumbfounded they stand;
When a voice so familiar is heard close at hand.
    (WIDOW TWANKY *is heard off-stage singing* "My old man . . ." *etc. She enters and comes to front of stage.*)
TWANKY. 'ere we are again. Still 'appy and cheerful are you? That's right. Now a very funny thing 'appened to me on the way to the palace tonight— (*Looking round.*) on the way to the . . . 'ere, where *is* the palace, eh? It was 'ere this morning because I came to collect the washing; and now I've brought it back and there ain't no palace to bring it to! (*To* GENIE.) I believe you've 'ad something to do with this, 'aven't you?
GENIE. I fear your unscrupulous brother has got
The palace, the Lamp, Lady Shoo-Shine—the lot.
TWANKY. Well, what a carry-on, eh? What a blooming turn-up! That Abanazar always was a naughty old lad. Well, now, Mr. Genie, I reckon you'd better fetch 'em all back again, right quick.
GENIE. Your request is impossible, madam, you see
I obey the Lamp's holder, whoever he be.
TWANKY (*sidling up to him*). Oh, I know all about that, ducky, but I reckon you could make an exception this time, couldn't you? (GENIE *shakes head.*) Oh, go on, be a sport—just to please me. (GENIE *shakes head again.*) 'ere, I tell you what—if you bring 'em back, I'll give that Abanazar what for, and I'll see he never bothers you again. Wonderful lamp, indeed! I'll lamp him all right. (GENIE *seems to hesitate.*) Look here, I'll make you a real tempting offer: if you bring the palace back, I'll promise to speak in verse for you. There; how's that? (*Speaking in deliberate verse.*)
Help me and I promise to mend my bad ways
And speak only in rhyme for the rest of my days.
I couldn't say fairer than that, Mr. Genie;
Oh, go on and do it now, don't be a meanie.
GENIE. I'm tempted. You swear there'll be no hanky-panky?
TWANKY. I promise, as sure as my name's Widow Twanky.
GENIE. It's a bargain! Let palace return now!
    (*Blackout, whistling noise, lights on.* UNCLE *and* SHOO-SHINE *have returned—with furniture.*)
SHOO-SHINE.   My mother!
EMPRESS. My daughter!

SHOO-SHINE. My Albert!
ALBERT (*embracing her*). My Shoo-Shine!
TWANKY (*holding* UNCLE's *ear and taking Lamp*). My brother!
UNCLE. Hey, you can't do this.
TWANKY. That's just one of your fallacies.
I'll teach you to run off with other folk's palaces.
GENIE. Madam, *you* hold the Lamp now. Command me, I pray.
TWANKY (*handing lamp to* GENIE).
'ere, you take it—and keep the thing out of harm's way.
GENIE. Thus, dear mortals, the Lamp is extinguished at last;
My job as its Slave is now over and past.
Young Laddin is happy, his bride is content;
The Empress is smiling; (*Indicating* UNCLE.) and as for this gent,
I suggest that we send him round second-class halls
To do conjuring tricks for the folk in the stalls.
   (UNCLE *performs a rapid conjuring trick.*)
Well, he had to do that one. We couldn't avoid it.
And so ends our show. We all hope you've enjoyed it.
Now go home and see that your lamps all shine bright;
As Al Laddin and company bid you:
ALL. Good night!

CURTAIN

Ask a Silly Question

A Panel-Game Minidrama

Richard Tydeman

A Samuel French Acting Edition

FOUNDED 1830

SAMUELFRENCH-LONDON.CO.UK
SAMUELFRENCH.COM

CHARACTERS

in the order of their appearance

Lady Faux-Parr, *the Chairman*
Mrs. Block, *a determined mother*
Mrs. Ambidex, *the caretaker*
Miss Trigg, *the mathematics mistress*
The Hon. Mrs. Landskip, *captain of the parents*
Mlle Plume-Tante, *French and music*
Mrs. Proliff, *mother of seven*
Miss Hurdlefast, *games and athletics*

also

Mrs. Ogilvy
Mrs. Quayle
Mrs. Ramsholt
Mrs. Shoolered
} *who ask the questions*

and a few voices from the audience

Scene: A meeting of the Parent Teachers Association in a local hall.

ASK A SILLY QUESTION

On the stage or platform are seven chairs, the centre one for the Chairman with a small table in front of it, and three chairs on each side. LADY FAUX-PARR *takes the centre chair and addresses the audience.*

LADY F-P. Good evening, good evening, and welcome to the special jubilee meeting of the High School Parent Teachers Association. Tonight, instead of a talk or a demonstration, we are to have a sort of quiz or brains trust of parents and members of the staff. I have been asked to act as Question Master because, of course, as Chairman of the Governors, I have nothing to do with the children or with the school. I do hope you are going to enjoy it. Now, are you sitting comfortably? Oh no, that's the wrong programme, isn't it. Still, it's a good question all the same. Hands up anyone who isn't comfortable.

(MRS. BLOCK, *near the front, puts up her hand.*)

Oh, what's the matter then?

BLOCK. There's something stuck to my seat. I think it's a caramel or a bit of chewing-gum or something.

LADY F-P. Oh dear, we can't have that. Is the caretaker there, please? Mrs. Ambidex—Mrs. Ambidex!

AMBIDEX (*from back of hall*). I'm here.

LADY F-P. Could you please do something about this lady's seat? I mean the one she's sitting on of course, and not the—oh well, you know what I mean.

AMBIDEX (*mumbling as she walks forward*). I'd like to do something about— (*The rest is indecipherable.*)

LADY F-P. What was that?

AMBIDEX. Nothing. (*She examines* MRS. BLOCK'S *chair.*)

LADY F-P. Well, can you find anything?

AMBIDEX. A great lump of toffee.

LADY F-P. Disgusting. I am so sorry, ladies. That's the worst of having to use a public hall for our meeting. It was probably left by somebody who used the hall yesterday. Who was here yesterday, Mrs. Ambidex?

AMBIDEX. The Parish Council. (*Or* "The Deacons' Meeting", *or something equally well known and unlikely to eat toffee.*)

LADY F-P. Oh well, I expect it could have been there for several days.

AMBIDEX. No, it couldn't. I clean this hall regular.

LADY F-P. Of course. Would you like to bring the toffee here?

AMBIDEX (*returning to back of hall*). No, I wouldn't.

LADY F-P. Perhaps you are right. And now, after that interruption, we had better proceed. Our panel tonight consists of three members of the staff and three parents, and I am going to introduce each one as I call her name. First the captains. On the school side we have Miss Trigg. Will you come up, please?

ASK A SILLY QUESTION

(MISS TRIGG *mounts platform and sits on Chairman's* L.)
Miss Trigg is the mathematics mistress. (*Consults notes.*) She is M.A. and M.B.E. and T.D. T.D.? What a very unusual distinction for a lady. Oh no, it's all right, that's my own abbreviation for "tone deaf", to remind me not to ask you any musical questions. (*Introducing.*) Miss Trigg.
TRIGG. Good evening. I would like to say—
LADY F-P. Thank you Miss Trigg. And now the captain of the parents: The Honourable Mrs. Landskip. Come along Mrs. Landskip, dear.
(MRS. LANDSKIP *mounts platform and sits on Chairman's right.*)
Mrs. Landskip is a neighbour of mine, and a great gardener. She has a daughter at the school, of course, and two very lively little boys who like to be Red Indians. I often look at them playing in the garden and think of the words of that lovely hymn which seem so appropriate: "Where every prospect pleases—" Mrs. Landskip.
LANDSKIP. My children are just as good—
LADY F-P. —as they can be. Yes, yes. Now, batting second for the staff is the French mistress, Mademoiselle Plume-Tante.
(MLLE PLUME-TANTE *sits* L. *of* MISS TRIGG.)
She also teaches music and dancing. She is L.R.A.M. and bar. No, no, L.R.A.M. and B.A., A.R.C.M., and a member of the Conservatory of Paris. No doubt that would be a degree in horticulture?
MLLE. In point of fact, Madame—
LADY F-P. Just as I thought. Now, in second place for the parents: Mrs. Proliff.
(MRS. PROLIFF *takes seat on* R. *of* MRS. LANDSKIP.)
Mrs. Proliff has five children, and seven of them are at the school. No, that must be vice versa.
PROLIFF. Actually it's Bertha and Elsie—
LADY F-P. I thought it must be. Bringing up the rear for the teachers is Miss Hurdlefast.
(MISS HURDLEFAST *sits extreme* L.)
Games mistress, editor of the school magazine, and a very witty speaker. At the university she was a half-blue for lacrosse and a half-blue for athletics, and I'm quite sure that if the university gave blues for wit, she would have been a half-blue for that as well.
HURDLEFAST. I hardly think—
LADY F-P. Oh, you're much too modest, dear. We shall look forward to many a good laugh at you later. And now, last but by no means least, for the parents, Mrs. Ambidex.
AMBIDEX(*from back of hall*). No, not me.
LADY F-P. But, Mrs. Ambidex, I have you on my list.
AMBIDEX. Then you can take me off again. There's plenty of others.
LADY F-P (*taken aback*). Oh, I don't know. I mean, who could we get to—
A VOICE FROM THE AUDIENCE. I would be willing—

ASK A SILLY QUESTION

ANOTHER VOICE. So would I.
BLOCK. What you need is someone with a bit of common sense.
LADY F-P. One at a time, please. Now perhaps as this lady had the misfortune to sit on a piece of toffee—what is your name, dear?
BLOCK. Mrs. Block.
LADY F-P. Then I suggest we give Mrs. Block a seat on the platform.
    (MRS. BLOCK *mounts platform and sits extreme* R.)
I haven't any notes about Mrs. Block, so perhaps she had better introduce herself.
BLOCK. My name is Mrs. Block. I have a daughter in the sixth form who is studying economics and wants to be a politician.
LADY F-P. Splendid. I'm sure your daughter is a chip off the old—er—following in your footsteps. Well now, ladies, that's the two teams. May we have the first question, please?
    (MRS. OGILVY *rises from the audience, advances to the foot of the platform and reads from a piece of paper.*)
MRS. OGILVY. Should girls in the higher forms of the school be compelled to wear uniform?
LADY F-P. Should girls in the higher forms of the school be compelled to wear uniform. Now, who's going to answer that one? Miss Trigg?
TRIGG. Certainly, certainly.
LADY F-P (*after a pause*). Do you mean, certainly they should, or certainly you will answer the question?
TRIGG. Both.
LADY F-P. Oh. Well, that's a nice short answer. Can we have the parents' view?
BLOCK. Ridiculous. Great girls dressed up like little kids with silly hats stuck on the tops of their heads. I'm all against it.
MLLE. The uniform can be most attractive if worn with a flair. The little summer dress, it is very chic.
PROLIFF. But who wants them to be attractive at that age? They are much too young.
BLOCK. Speak for yourself. Many girls of seventeen are married these days.
LADY F-P. But Mrs. Proliff is more than seventeen.
BLOCK. Her eldest is the same age as mine.
HURDLEFAST. The best thing is to concentrate on games. Uniform is essential for a real team spirit.
BLOCK. Games develop all the wrong muscles.
HURDLEFAST. Nonsense.
LADY F-P. Now, we haven't yet heard from the captain of the parents. What do you think, Mrs. Landskip dear?
LANDSKIP. What was the question?
LADY F-P. Should girls—
    (MRS. LANDSKIP *puts a hand to her ear.*)

A.S.Q.*

3

Can you hear me, dear?

LANDSKIP. Not very well. This is my bad ear. Do you think I could come on the other side?

LADY F-P. Oh, I'm so sorry. Yes, of course. Miss Trigg, would you mind changing places?

TRIGG. Not at all.

(*They change.*)

LADY F-P. That's better.

TRIGG. Excuse me, but in order to keep the teams together, wouldn't it be better if we all changed?

LADY F-P. Perhaps it would. Do you mind, ladies?

(MRS. PROLIFF *and* MRS. BLOCK *change places with* MLLE PLUME-TANTE *and* MISS HURDLEFAST.)

Good, good, that's divided the sheep from the goats, but don't ask me which is which. Now, may we have the next question, please?

(MRS. QUAYLE *advances and reads from a paper.*)

MRS. QUAYLE. Does the team agree that homework should be abolished?

LADY F-P. Ah; does the team agree—

BLOCK. Yes.

TRIGG. No.

LADY F-P. Well, that seems to be the answer to that one. The team does not agree.

LANDSKIP. What was the question?

LADY F-P (*in her ear*). Does the team agree that homework should be abolished?

LANDSKIP. Oh, I see. Thank you.

LADY F-P (*after a pause*). Were you wanting to say anything?

LANDSKIP. Me? No, I don't think so. Was I?

BLOCK. Well, if Mrs. Landskip doesn't want to say anything, I do. Every night from six till ten, can I have the telly on? No. Can I listen to the radio? No. Can I talk? No.

LADY F-P. That must be a great hardship for you.

BLOCK. All the evening we have to sit in stony silence just because of homework. (*She points at* MISS TRIGG.) And that one's the worst. She sets my Gladys enough sums to keep a bank clerk busy for a week.

TRIGG. If your daughter wishes to pass her examination—

BLOCK. Find the sum of the difference between the square root of x and y, and express your answer in centimetres.

LADY F-P. Thank you, Mrs. Block.

BLOCK. Draw a graph showing the rise in population in Bradford between the wars.

TRIGG. I can assure you—

BLOCK. If it takes a hen and a half a day and a half to lay an egg and a half, how long would it take a cross-eyed bloater to swim across a barrel of treacle.

TRIGG. Now, that is just being ridiculous.
LADY F-P (*writing*). Wait a minute, I think I know the answer to that one. A hen and a half—
                (MRS. LANDSKIP *starts writing, too.*)
HURDLEFAST. Madam Chairman, may I say a word, please. There is no doubt at all that homework is a serious drawback to the school's athletic progress. At the time when a girl should be out training for the inter-house match she has to sit at home in a stuffy, badly ventilated, insufficiently lighted room—
PROLIFF. Oh no, I can assure you our house isn't stuffy, and we had special lights fitted for all the children. I am in favour of homework. (*She sighs.*) It's the only time I get a bit of peace and quiet.
MLLE. If homework is made interesting, the girls will like it. Those who learn the piano—
BLOCK. The piano! Don't talk to me about the piano. Don't talk to me.
MLLE. Well, I wasn't.
BLOCK. I live, as you possibly know, next door to Mrs. Ambidex, and her daughter has been playing about with that Merry Peasant all the term.
AMBIDEX (*from back of hall*). She's better than your Gladys and the Chocolate Soldier.
BLOCK. My Gladys is a virtuoso.
AMBIDEX. I wasn't criticizing her morals.
TRIGG. Madam Chairman!
LADY F-P (*still writing*). Yes, dear? Just a minute, I've nearly got it, but I can't see why the bloater has to be cross-eyed.
HURDLEFAST. All bloaters are cross-eyed.
LADY F-P. Are they? Well, yes, now you come to mention it, I believe they are.
AMBIDEX (*singing*). "Come, come, I love you only—"
PROLIFF. Madam Chairman, may I suggest that Mrs. Ambidex be invited to come up on the platform and give her views?
LADY F-P. Yes, yes, of course.
BLOCK. Oh no, she's had her chance and she wouldn't take it.
                (*They all argue and talk at once.*)
LADY F-P (*banging on table*). Please, please, please. (*Silence.*) Mrs. Ambidex, would you care to come up?
AMBIDEX. No, thanks. I'll stay down here with the merry peasants.
LADY F-P. In that case, perhaps we'd better have another question. Who's next?
                (MRS. RAMSHOLT *advances and reads.*)
MRS. RAMSHOLT. Do the members of the panel approve of girls having boy friends while they are still at school?
PROLIFF. No, I do not.
LADY F-P. Just a minute please, while I repeat the question. Do the members of the panel—

ASK A SILLY QUESTION

BLOCK. We all heard it the first time.
LADY F-P. Oh, did you? But perhaps everybody didn't. Mrs. Landskip dear, did you hear the question?
LANDSKIP (*looking up from writing*). What question?
LADY F-P (*to* MRS. BLOCK). There you are, you see. (*To* MRS. LANDSKIP.) Do the members of the panel approve of girls having boy friends while they are still at school.
LANDSKIP. When who are still at school, the girls or the boy friends? (*She resumes her writing.*)
HURDLEFAST. Or the members of the panel?
TRIGG. Personally I have never been bothered by boy friends.
BLOCK. Bad luck, mate.
TRIGG. I just set the girls enough homework to keep them really busy. There's nothing like a good bit of homework—
BLOCK. That's what the boy friends say.
LADY F-P. Mrs. Block, I must ask you to give the other members a chance to speak. Now, Mlle Plume-Tante, what are your views on boy friends?
MLLE. Well, of course in France—
BLOCK. Keep it clean.
MLLE. —the problem does not arise, because the girls and boys mix together from a very early age.
BLOCK. That's not all they do, from what I hear.
LADY F-P. Mrs. Block!
PROLIFF. There is one little girl that I see regularly; she can't be more than fourteen, and she walks arm in arm with that boy from the pet shop.
BLOCK. Oh well, you know who that is, don't you? That's young Anthea Ambidex. Cheeky hussy.
AMBIDEX. You leave my Anthea alone.
BLOCK. Try telling that to the boy from the pet shop.
HURDLEFAST. Madam Chairman, is this true?
LADY F-P. I don't know, dear.
HURDLEFAST. I want Anthea in the first eleven next term, Mrs. Ambidex. You mustn't let anything stand in her way.
AMBIDEX. My Anthea's all right.
BLOCK. That's what the boy from the pet shop says.
AMBIDEX. I haven't noticed any boys wanting to take your Gladys out.
BLOCK. My Gladys gets on with her work.
AMBIDEX. Work! Politician my foot.
LADY F-P. Mrs. Ambidex, it really would be more convenient if you could come and express your views on the platform.
AMBIDEX. No, thank you. If my family is going to be insulted, you can come and insult us down here at the back.
LADY F-P (*sighing*). Oh dear. I think we'd better change the subject and go on to another question. Yes, please?

(Mrs. SHOOLBRED *advances and reads in an expressionless monotone.*)

MRS. SHOOLBRED. In view of the increasing need for production especially in the export market and taking into consideration the accelerated pace of modern living, would the team be inclined to think or perhaps to disagree with the idea that there is not sufficient pride taken by school-leavers in the various forms of employment for which their education has inadequately equipped them, and if so would they care to suggest the underlying causes for this situation and to suggest any ways in which a remedy might be applied to prevent the continued recurrence of what has come to be recognized as one of the major problems of our time.

LADY F-P. Good gracious. I'm afraid I can't possibly repeat that question, and I don't really know what it means.

BLOCK. It means, why don't people work as hard as they used to.

HURDLEFAST. Now, that's a much better question. And the answer is, because they don't take enough exercise.

PROLIFF. They have too much time and too much money.

TRIGG. They get too much entertainment and not enough discipline.

LANDSKIP (*putting down her pencil and picking up paper*). There now, I think I have the answer to that one.

LADY F-P. Oh, good.

LANDSKIP. Yes, you see it's a catch question, but I didn't see it at first. And the catch is, of course, that bloaters can't swim.

LADY F-P. Bloaters?

LANDSKIP. Yes, you see the fish that swims is called a herring. It's not called a bloater until after it's dead. Oh, that's very good. I must try and remember that.

MLLE. Could we perhaps return to the question now?

BLOCK. Hear, hear. Madam Chairman, this is by far the most serious question we have had so far, and it deserves a serious answer. People do not work as hard these days as they used to. This doesn't just apply to young people but to older ones as well. We none of us work as hard as we should.

AMBIDEX. You speak for yourself!

BLOCK. Oh, I do, I do.

HURDLEFAST. But surely that's not a bad thing in itself. Modern machinery is designed to give us more leisure. The real problem is what we do with our leisure. If we spent more time out in the open air—

BLOCK. We have no business to enjoy leisure at all unless all our work is done first.

LADY F-P. But, Mrs. Block, can you give us an example of work that is not being done properly?

BLOCK. Oh, I'm not one to criticize, but— (*She looks round.*) Take this hall for example.

AMBIDEX. Careful!
BLOCK. Now, without being too critical, could you call it clean?
AMBIDEX. Clean? Why, you could eat off the floor.
BLOCK (*studying floor*). It looks as though somebody has.
AMBIDEX (*advancing half-way up the hall*). That is a deliberate and uncalled-for lie.
LADY F-P. Please, please. I am sure that Mrs. Block was speaking metaphorically.
BLOCK. I might, if I knew what that meant. But I can recognize dirt when I see it. (*She rubs her finger along the Chairman's table and looks at it.*) Filthy!
AMBIDEX. There's not a speck of dust on that table, Mrs. Block, and you know it.
BLOCK. Madam Chairman, I appeal to you.
LADY F-P (*rubbing her finger on table and looking at it*). Well, now you come to mention it—
   (*She shows her finger to* MISS TRIGG, *who rubs her own finger on table and shows it to the others. They all rub their fingers and show them to each other, shaking their heads sadly.*)
I'm afraid Mrs. Block is right, you know.
AMBIDEX (*advancing*). I don't believe a word of it.
   (*She mounts platform. The others exchange pleased glances.*)
Now, show me your fingers.
BLOCK. We've wiped them clean now.
AMBIDEX (*rubbing her own finger on table and showing it*). Look here; clean as a whistle.
LADY F-P (*rising*). I think, round this side—
   (MRS. AMBIDEX *moves round.*)
Here now, you just sit down in my chair and look along the surface of the table and you will see.
   (MRS. AMBIDEX *sits. At once,* LADY FAUX-PARR *stands behind her and puts both hands on her shoulders as if to hold her down.*)
AMBIDEX. Here, what's the game?
LADY F-P. Members of the audience, we owe you an apology. We have been asking silly questions and getting silly answers because it was the only way we could achieve our object. It has taken us nearly half an hour, but we've done it. I told you this was a special jubilee meeting, and so it is. Tonight we have a big surprise for you: the television cameras are waiting in the wings— (*A bright light could shine from wings on to stage.*) and so, Mrs. Ambidex, mother, housewife, Red Cross worker, for twenty-five years caretaker of this building— This Is Your Life!
   (*She produces a large book—or, better still, a man enters bearing a large book. If possible a television cameraman appears, and all close in on* MRS. AMBIDEX *as the* CURTAIN *falls. If there is no curtain available, or if the producer prefers, an alternative ending would be for* MRS.

ASK A SILLY QUESTION

AMBIDEX *to jump up, exclaiming, "Oh no, it isn't!" and march off down through the audience, followed by the entire cast all calling to her and pleading at the tops of their voices.)*

PRODUCTION NOTE

This minidrama is a "conversation piece", specially designed for presentation in halls with very small platforms or no platform at all, and it can be put on with the minimum of preparation.

Seven chairs and a table are the only furniture required, and no special costumes or scenery will be needed. There is little movement, and it would be quite easy for most of the players to have a copy of the script among their papers and notes, if desired.

Production should, therefore, present few difficulties. The important thing is for each player to establish her own individual character. LADY FAUX-PARR has the knack of "putting her foot into it" at frequent intervals, entirely without malice, moving onwards like a benevolent steam-roller. Each of the team, parents and teachers, should be well contrasted. MRS. BLOCK might effectively have a strong regional accent. MRS. AMBIDEX, who might be called the "heroine" of the piece, is obviously shy of coming forward, but confident enough when she can make remarks from the back. The ladies who ask questions should come out of their places to the front, read their questions, and return to their seats. Finally, of course, there should be no hint at all of the real purpose of the meeting, until the last speech.   R.T.

FIESTA FANDANGO

A "Spanish Minidrama"

by

RICHARD TYDEMAN

Samuel French – London
New York – Sydney – Toronto – Hollywood

CHARACTERS

The Compère, *who has the book of words*
Rosina, *a sweet Señorita*
Don Lopez, *her not so sweet father*
Rodrigo, *a dark and handsome valet*
Dolores
Netta   } *enterprising maids*
Tessa
Magdalena
Inez, *Rosina's Duenna*
Don Carlos Gonzales Paralos, *a wealthy suitor*

SCENE: a room in the house of Don Lopez
(Production Note at end of play)

COPYRIGHT INFORMATION
(See also page ii)

This play is fully protected under the Copyright Laws of the British Commonwealth of Nations, the United States of America and all countries of the Berne and Universal Copyright Conventions.

All rights, including Stage, Motion Picture, Radio, Television, Public Reading, and Translation into Foreign Languages, are strictly reserved.

No part of this publication may lawfully be reproduced in ANY form or by any means — photocopying, typescript, recording (including video-recording), manuscript, electronic, mechanical, or otherwise — or be transmitted or stored in a retrieval system, without prior permission.

Rights of Performance by Amateurs are controlled by Samuel French Ltd, 52 Fitzroy Street, London W1P 6JR, and they, or their authorized agents, issue licences to amateurs on payment of a fee. **It is an infringement of the Copyright to give any performance or public reading of the play before the fee has been paid and the licence issued.**

Licences are issued subject to the understanding that it shall be made clear in all advertising matter that the audience will witness an amateur performance; that the names of the authors of the plays shall be included on all announcements and on all programmes; and that the integrity of the authors' work will be preserved.

The Royalty Fee is subject to contract and subject to variation at the sole discretion of Samuel French Ltd.

In Theatres or Halls seating Four Hundred or more the fee will be subject to negotiation.

In Territories Overseas the fee quoted in this Acting Edition may not apply. A fee will be quoted on application to our local authorized agent, or if there is no such agent, on application to Samuel French Ltd, London.

VIDEO RECORDING OF AMATEUR PRODUCTIONS

Please note that the copyright laws governing video-recording are extremely complex and that it should not be assumed that any play may be video-recorded for *whatever purpose* without first obtaining the permission of the appropriate agents. The fact that a play is published by Samuel French Ltd does not indicate that video rights are available or that Samuel French Ltd controls such rights.

FIESTA FANDANGO

The COMPERE *appears before the curtain dressed in vaguely Spanish costume, possibly with a guitar slung over one shoulder, and a copy of the script in his hand.*

COMPERE. Señoras so gay, and Señors, good day;
I hope you are listening well,
For I'm here to beguile your thoughts for a while,
And I want you to hear what I tell.
But in fact or in fiction, the clearest of diction
I always attempt to maintain;
So cease from siesta, and join our Fiesta
Fandango from fictional Spain.
On the side of a hill near the town of Seville
Lives Rosina, a sweet señorita;
But she hasn't much hope as her father, Don Lopez,
Will not permit young men to meet her.
So day after day in her room she must stay
Feeling thoroughly left on the shelf;
I tell you for certain—but ring up the curtain
And see the young lady herself.

(*The curtain rises showing* ROSINA *sitting disconsolate in her room, which can be as elaborate or as simple as you like.*)

There she is. What a beauty! I feel it my duty
To tell you she's only eighteen;
And think what she's missed, for she's never been kissed.
ROSINA. I really don't know what you mean.
What is it,—this kissing that I have been missing?
COMPERE. It's not very easy to say.
I could *show* you,—but there, I suppose a compère
Mustn't really take part in the play.
And there's no time for more, as we see at the door
Don Lopez himself with his train:
A regular ballet of maids, and a valet,
The finest assortment in Spain.

FIESTA FANDANGO

(*Enter* DON LOPEZ, *with his valet* RODRIGO, *and his four maids,* TESSA, NETTA, DOLORES *and* MAGDALENA.)

LOPEZ. Good morning my child.
COMPERE.   Says the Don, and he smiled,—
  Did you notice his smile, as he said it?
  For this grandee is quite the most strictly polite;
  Let that much be said to his credit.
  His theme he pursues:
LOPEZ.   I bring happiest news,
COMPERE. (And gravely he bows to salute her.)
LOPEZ. For I've promised your hand, and the half of my land,
  To a highly desirable suitor.
COMPERE. Upon hearing him speak, Rosina turns weak,
  And looking decidedly dizzy,
  Recovers at length, and summons up strength
  To inquire in a whisper:
ROSINA.   Who is he?
LOPEZ. He is,
COMPERE.   Says her sire,
LOPEZ.   All the heart can desire;
  He has wealth and position and knowledge.
  His name is Don Carlos Gonzalez Paralos,—
  My best friend at Cordova College.
ROSINA. But father, dear father, I'd very much rather
  I married a man of my own age.
  If you took your B.A. on the very same day,
  Don Carlos dates back to the Stone Age!

(DON LOPEZ *raises a hand for silence.*)

COMPERE. That wave of the hand, you will quite understand,
  Puts a stop to all further discussion.

(*Exit* DON LOPEZ. *The Maids follow.*)

  Off goes the grandee with his train,
ROSINA.   Leaving me
  The victim of mental concussion.
COMPERE. But wait: for although the rest of them go,
  Rodrigo seems anxious to tarry.
RODRIGO. My lady, so madly I love you, that gladly
  I'll die, if that old man you marry! (*He seizes her hand.*)
COMPERE. Such a bold declaration from one of low station

Has knocked our young heroine flat.
> (ROSINA *shrinks back.*)

And its suddenness, too—coming out of the blue,
> (RODRIGO *starts to turn away.*)

But none the less welcome for that.
> (ROSINA *pulls him back again.*)

ROSINA. Do you mean it?
RODRIGO. My dear, ever since I came here
  I have loved you with passion so free,
  That if you are wed, I would rather be dead—
  Unless you are wedded to me.
COMPERE. All girls think it bliss to hear rubbish like this,
  And she hopes he will never be done;
  As he pours in her ear those sweet nothings you hear
  If you sit in the back row but one.
  Then he shows her what I was quite willing to try,
  And he kisses her once, and then twice—
  And she doesn't resist. Well there, now you've been kissed,
  Tell me, how do you like it?
ROSINA (*emerging from an embrace*). It's nice.
> (*The embrace continues.*)

COMPERE. It is evident quite, we shall be here all night
  If we don't make a move in a hurry.
  Now look here, young man, you will need a good plan.
RODRIGO (*producing papers from his pocket*).
  I've got one already. Don't worry.
COMPERE. Well, I really must say, this unusual valet
  Could never be labelled as sloppy.
RODRIGO. Before I forget it; I'd like you to vet it—
  Allow me to hand you a copy.
> (*He hands* COMPERE *a typed sheet, and then walks slowly off with his arm round* ROSINA *as* COMPERE *continues:*)

COMPERE. With that, the young pair, saying good-bye to care,
  Not giving a thought for their seniors,
  Go off to inspect how the moon's rays reflect
  On the fountains among the gardenias.
  Which is awkward for me, because as you see
  The stage is now empty and void.
  But here comes Rosina's Duenna, old Inez,

I fancy she's rather annoyed.
> (*Enter* INEZ, *the Duenna.*)

INEZ. Oh, what a disaster! I hear that the master
Is planning to marry Rosina
To wealthy Don Carlos Gonzalez Paralos,
And Carlos has not even seen her!
COMPERE. And what, pray, are you intending to do
To save the young maid from the Don?
INEZ. I have thought of a plan. Here you are, my good man,
> (*Handing him a typed sheet.*)

You can read it yourself when I've gone. (*Exit into garden.*)
COMPERE. Well, this is amazing. I find I am gazing
At two people's plans in proximity;
And they both at the top say "This marriage must stop".
That's remarkably fine unanimity.
> (*Enter* DON CARLOS. *He coughs to attract attention.*)

CARLOS. Ahem.
COMPERE. What the dickens? Aha, the plot thickens;
I think I need hardly explain
That here is Don Carlos Gonzalez Paralos—
Ten thousand a year, and no brain. (*Turns and bows to* DON CARLOS.)
CARLOS. I've come here to meet a refined Señorita;
Where is she?
COMPERE.   Don Carlos, your pardon—
(*Aside.*) Oh dear, what a fix! (*Aloud.*) She won't be two ticks,
She is taking a walk in the garden.
CARLOS. I'll join her.
COMPERE (*quickly*).   No, no; there's no need to go;
I fancy I hear her returning.
CARLOS (*calling*). Rosina!
INEX (*off*).   Yoo-hoo!
CARLOS.   I am waiting for you.
> (*Re-enter* INEZ, *with arms outstretched.*)

INEZ. No wonder my ears have been burning!
> (INEZ *embraces* CARLOS. *He escapes and addresses* COMPERE.)

CARLOS. I was told she was pretty, and youthful and witty;
Was ever a man so deceived!
Now I find she's a fat one.
(*Re-enter* ROSINA.)   I'd rather have *that* one.

COMPERE. Don Carlos, you mustn't look grieved:
A woman who cooks is worth two with good looks.
INEZ. We'll be married as soon as you say.
But first I must send—my maid—(*To* ROSINA.) please pretend,
And keep father out of the way.
> (ROSINA *smiles understandingly and goes out.* INEZ *takes* CARLOS *by the arm.*)

COMPERE. What these two discuss doesn't need concern us,
So we'll just draw the curtain a minute,
> (*Curtain falls, leaving* COMPERE *outside.*)

And look at the plan of that pleasant young man—
I'll read you a bit of what's in it:
> (*Reading from first typed sheet.*)

"A ladder I'll bring at midnight and sing
Selections from Strauss Operettas.
Rosina will hear my song and appear
Disguised as a sack of potatoes!"
> (*Breaking off in disgust.*)

I know that at times it is hard to find rhymes,
But atrocious as these verses are—
To rhyme "operettas" with "sack of potettas",
Atrocity's carried too far!
But now he goes on: "To escape from the Don
I'll carry the sack to my digs,
And pretend I'm a peasant of aspect unpleasant
Who's taking some spuds to his pigs".
> (*Breaking off again.*)

I know I'm pedantic, but how unromantic!
> (*The head of* DON CARLOS *appears round the curtain.* COMPERE *does not see him.*)

CARLOS. I'll spoil this young Romeo's joke;
Before he comes back, I'll run off with that sack.
> (*The head disappears.*)

COMPERE. Eh? (*Turning.*) I'm sorry; I thought someone spoke.
Now I'd better just read old Inez's screed:
> (*Reading from the other typed sheet.*)

"I always look under the bed,
In case there's a man—" What a very odd plan!
> (INEZ *appears, takes the paper and hands him another.*)

INEZ. I've changed it. Read this one instead. (*Exit.*)
COMPERE (*reading the new paper*).
"I'm sure that Don C. would do better with me,
So I'll stay by the ladder all night;
And before he comes back, like proverbial Jack,
I'll remove it, and *I'll* be all right!"
(*Re-enter* RODRIGO.)
RODRIGO. I've altered my mind. Enclosed you will find
A much better plan than the first.
(*Hands* COMPERE *a paper and goes out.*)
COMPERE. Well, really, I find this a trifle unkind.
Still, I might as well read you the worst:
(*Reading from* RODRIGO'S *latest paper.*)
"Don Carlos has rumbled my plan and has stumbled
On what you were formerly told;
So I'll leave him to make his biggest mistake,
And substitute pewter for gold:
When the sack is untied he'll find Inez inside,
Which will serve the old perisher right.
Please pass on this letter to Tessa and Netta,
And tell them Tonight Is The Night."
I'm afraid that I fail to make head or tail
Of this incomprehensible text.
But it's nearly midnight, so I think that we might
Raise the curtain, and see what comes next.
(*Curtain rises on the same scene, but it is now midnight. The four maids,* TESSA, NETTA, DOLORES, *and* MAGDALENA, *are discovered in picturesque attitudes.*)
Hullo, what's all this? Now pardon me, miss,
But will you please say who you are?
DOLORES. I'm Dolores.
NETTA.   I'm Netta.
TESSA.   I'm Tessa.
COMPERE.   That's better;
I'm asked to give this to you.
MAGDALENA (*taking paper from him*). Ta.
COMPERE. I wonder if you will know what to do?
They carefully read it together.
Yes, they certainly know: for two of them go,
(*Exeunt* TESSA *and* NETTA.)

While the other two talk of the weather:
DOLORES. On the mountain tonight, the moon's shining bright.
MAGDALENA. The ice is beginning to thaw.
DOLORES. The rain in Spain stays mainly on the plain.
COMPERE. Now where have I heard that before?
Hullo, here comes Tess.
(*Re-enter* TESSA, *followed by* NETTA.)
MAGDALENA. Have you managed it?
TESSA. Yes.
NETTA. I'm afraid that we had to use force.
TESSA. Just a touch with my cosh, and she passed out.
DOLORES. Oh, gosh!
I hope she's still breathing?
TESSA. Of course.
But Inez is tough, and we had to get rough,
And it's dark, and she would keep on shifting.
NETTA. Still she's in the sack and—if you'll give us a hand—
"The potatoes are ready for lifting".
(*They all laugh, and help carry on a sack containing someone. They deposit sack* C., *preferably upright, so that the occupant is the right way up.*)
COMPERE. Now you'd all better hide. Let's have two on each side.
(*Two "hide"* D.L., *and two* D.R.)
For midnight approaches apace.
(*Twelve rapid strokes of a bell, off.*)
As the twelve strokes we hear, at the window appear
A hand, then an arm, then a face.
(*Enter* DON CARLOS, *cautiously. He sees the sack.*)
CARLOS. Aha, I'm in luck. The dear little duck
Is waiting for me to embrace her.
(*With arms round the sack.*)
My lovely, my dear, your Carlos is here.
(INEZ *enters behind him with open arms.*)
INEZ. Then turn round, my darling, and face her!
CARLOS. Carramba! (INEZ *embraces him, and they move* D.R.)
COMPERE. Well, well! We're saved by the bell.
But girls, what on earth have you done?
You have hit on the head Rosina instead.
NETTA. Oh, Tess!
TESSA (*tearful*). It was only in fun.
COMPERE. Well, get her out quick. That sack is so thick.

(*All four maids start to undo the sack.*)
MAGDALENA. Poor darling! We'll have to work fast.
(*Enter* RODRIGO. *He embraces the sack.*)
RODRIGO. Rosina, my love, my poor little dove,
Rosina!
(ROSINA *enters behind him with open arms.*)
ROSINA. Rodrigo, at last!
(*They embrace and move* D.L. *Consternation among the maids.*)
COMPERE. This is past all belief! With joy and relief
The maids by the sack give a sigh.
But wait just a minute! Who *have* you got in it?
(*The sack bursts open and* DON LOPEZ *emerges from it.*)
RODRIGO. Good heavens!
ROSINA.   Good gracious!
TESSA (*going*).   Good-bye!
LOPEZ. Come hither, you slut! I am murdered—all but.
Now explain this disgraceful attack.
COMPERE. Poor Tess is afraid. It's not often a maid
Can "give her employer the sack"!
But she's saved in the end:
LOPEZ (*suddenly catching sight of* CARLOS). Don Carlos, my friend!
COMPERE. And he bows—though a trifle unsteady.
LOPEZ. My daughter is here. (*He indicates* ROSINA.)
CARLOS (*moving towards her*). Good evening, my dear.
INEZ (*pulling* CARLOS *back*). Don Carlos is suited already.
LOPEZ. He is suited? (*To* ROSINA.) Then who can we marry to you?
COMPERE. Rosina steps up to her dad:
ROSINA. Oh, Father, let me go and marry Rodrigo.
LOPEZ. What? Marry my valet? You're mad!
COMPERE. But here's a surprise: this is only disguise;
He's not really your valet, I fear.
He's Santos Le Cid, the Kid from Madrid,
The Toreador of the year!
(RODRIGO *bows.*)
LOPEZ. A Toreador? My dear son-in-law! (*He shakes* RODRIGO's *hand.*)
COMPERE. His heart with delight is now full.
For what is a mere ten thousand per year
Compared with ten thousand per bull?
LOPEZ. My daughter I'll bless. I'll forgive even Tess—

In fact, if I marry again
I think, on my life, she would make a good wife.
> (*Rubbing the bruise on his head.*)

For her arm is the strongest in Spain.
> (*He embraces* TESSA.)

COMPERE. So Carlos gets Inez, Rodrigo's Rosina's,
And father is happy I know.
> (NETTA, DOLORES *and* MAGDALENA *gaze at* COMPERE.)

Which leaves us with three who are looking at me.
I'll see you girls after the show.
> (*To audience.*)

So ends our Fandango—so far as we can go;
Though it's not very Spanish, you say?
Well, maybe you're right; so we won't say Good Night,
But, "Adios, amigos. Olé!"
ALL (*with two stamps of the feet*). Olé!

CURTAIN

PRODUCTION NOTE

All Minidramas are designed to give the least possible trouble in rehearsal and presentation, but certain basic rules must be kept: each character must say the exact words as written, to preserve the rhythm of the atrocious verse, and where necessary the sense of the words must be sacrificed to the rhythm which is all-important. Entrances and exits must be slick, and at exactly the right time. The Compère should act as prompter.

Costumes are simple: a few Spanish-looking shawls, brightly coloured skirts, handkerchiefs, combs in the hair, moustaches for the men, and the atmosphere is created at once.

The atmosphere will also be helped by suitable music played before and afterwards. It might be a good idea to let the whole cast join in dancing a real fandango—or a cachuca or something, before the final curtain falls.

A note on the characters: The Compère is partly a storyteller, partly a commentator, and partly a character in the play. He can, if necessary, read his part. Rosina is young and pretty. Don Lopez, her father, is elderly and proud. Rodrigo should be dark and handsome, but if necessary he can be fair and handsome. The maids can be any age; Inez should be on the large side, and not too young. Don Carlos is the same age as Don Lopez, and is both wealthy and brainless.

The bare minimum of stage directions have been given in the text, and generally speaking when the Compère is describing the movements of other characters these movements have not been separately described in the directions.

The sack must be both large enough and thick enough to conceal the identity of its occupant; double thickness is recommended.

Forty Winks Beauty

A Potted Panto, Very Vaguely Based on
"The Sleeping Beauty"

Richard Tydeman

A Samuel French Acting Edition

SAMUELFRENCH-LONDON.CO.UK
SAMUELFRENCH.COM

CHARACTERS

The Compere
The King
The Queen
Leading Fairy
Second Fairy
Third Fairy

Maud, *a Wicked Fairy*
A Soldier
Beauty, *a Princess*
A Nurse
Charley
A Prince

Scene: The King's Palace

(Production Note at end of play)

© 1956 BY RICHARD TYDEMAN

Rights of Performance by Amateurs are controlled by Samuel French Ltd, 52 Fitzroy Street, London W1P 6JR, and they, or their authorized agents, issue licences to amateurs on payment of a fee. **It is an infringement of the Copyright to give any performance or public reading of the play before the fee has been paid and the licence issued.**

The Royalty Fee indicated below is subject to contract and subject to variation at the sole discretion of Samuel French Ltd.

Basic fee for each and every
performance by amateurs   Code B
in the British Isles

The publication of this play does not imply that it is necessarily available for performance by amateurs or professionals, either in the British Isles or Overseas. Amateurs and professionals considering a production are strongly advised in their own interests to apply to appropriate agents for consent before starting rehearsals or booking a theatre or hall.

ISBN 0 573 06616 7

FORTY WINKS BEAUTY

Act One

The Compere *appears before the curtain carrying a full copy of the script, to which he refers from time to time.*

Compere. Kind friends, as your announcer, it is now my pleasant duty
To introduce our Potted Panto, "Forty Winks for Beauty".
Our scene's the palace of the King of nowhere in particular,
(The floors are horizontal and the walls are perpendicular)
But more important far than all these solid bricks and mortar,
The King and Queen have organised a party for their daughter.

(Curtain up, revealing King *and* Queen *standing by cot, and three or more* Fairies.*)*

And round the small Princess's cot in dresses white and glistening,
The Fairies have all gathered with their presents for the christening.

Fairy 1. My present for the baby is a nature sweet and gentle,
And may she like all novels that are super-sentimental.

Fairy 2. I wish the baby goodness that will never need correction.

Fairy 3. And I wish she may ever have a *real* schoolgirl complexion.

King. We thank you, Fairies, kindly for your gifts and your good wishes.

Queen. And please accept with compliments these silver-plated dishes.

(Enter Maud, *a wicked Fairy, enveloped in a black cloak.)*

Compere. But who is this with face so fierce, and eyes as black as pitch?
It is the wicked fairy Maud, a nasty-tempered—witch.

Maud. Ho, ho! And so you thought you wouldn't ask me to the party.

King. We—thought that you were ill.

Maud   Oh no, I'm very hale and hearty.

FORTY WINKS BEAUTY

KING. Well, all the same, we're glad you came.
COMPERE (aside). Oh what a whopper!
KING (to QUEEN). Mabel, Just run and tell the maids to lay another place at table.
MAUD. And now I'd like a silver dish just like you gave the others.
QUEEN. Oh dear, oh dear, there *was* one here—
KING. I took it round to Mother's.
COMPERE. But Maud is in a temper now, and with a smile unpleasant, She turns towards the helpless babe and gives a fatal present:
MAUD. I wish your brat may prick her little finger on a spindle And die of slow blood-poisoning. Goodbye. (*She starts to go.*)
KING. Here, that's a swindle! We can't have that.
MAUD. Then put it in your pipe and have a smoke.
(*Goes out.*)
QUEEN. Oh, heavens above!
KING. Don't worry, love. It's just her little joke.
FAIRY 1. I sadly fear, your Majesty, it's not a joke, it's tragic.
KING. Well, can't you Fairies cancel out the spell with other magic?
COMPERE. The Fairies all look serious and go into a huddle, To see if they can find a good solution to the muddle. At last the leading Fairy speaks:
FAIRY 1. We cannot break the spell.
COMPERE. This Makes the King so mad.
KING. I wish old Maud would go to—
COMPERE. Well, The Fairies in the corner have another little natter, And then they say:
FAIRY 2. To break a spell is not an easy matter. Make no mistake, we cannot break this spell, and nor can you. But we can bend it quite a bit.
COMPERE. And that is what they do.
FAIRIES (*dancing in a ring*).
Eeny meeny, teeny weeny, shut the door and lock it.
Maskelyne and Robin Hood, John Bourne and Davy Crockett;

These are names to conjure with, as anyone can tell,
So here we call upon them all to help us bend the spell.
(They stop and put their heads together whispering. The KING *and* QUEEN *clasp each other in terror.)*

COMPERE. At last the Fairies straighten up, their magic task completed.
The leader speaks:

FAIRY 1. Your Majesty, old Maud is now defeated;
The Princess will not really die, in spite of all your fears,
But now instead she'll go to bed and sleep a hundred years.

QUEEN. A hundred years!

COMPERE. The Queen in tears upon the sofa sinks.
The King upon his fingers counts:

KING. That's forty *thousand* winks!

FAIRY 1. At your behest we've done our best, and there we'll have to stand.
So now, goodbye.

COMPERE. And off they fly, back home to Fairyland.
(Exeunt FAIRIES.*)*

(The KING *has been scribbling on a paper; he now claps his hands, and a* SOLDIER *enters.)*

The King now calls his Chief of Staff and gives him urgent orders.

KING. This proclamation go and make throughout our royal borders.

*(*SOLDIER *takes paper from* KING *and reads it.)*

SOLDIER. "Let every spindle, spinning wheel and sharply pointed thing,
Howe'er employed, be now destroyed. By Order. Signed, the King.
P.S. Whoever disobeys, or man, or maid, or wife,
Shall have his head cut off and then be sent to jail for life." *(Salutes and goes out.)*

COMPERE. So there we'll draw the curtain on the tragic royal pair;
And leave the little Princess crying:

BEAUTY *(off, in baby voice).* Nyair! Nyair! Nyair!

(The Curtain falls, leaving COMPERE *outside.)*

Act Two

COMPERE. The years have quickly rolled away, as years so often do;
So we'll exclude the interlude and pass on to Act Two.
The Princess has been growing fast, and I'm prepared to wager
In all your days you'll never gaze on such a cute teen-ager.

(*Curtain up. The cot has disappeared, and* BEAUTY *is sitting on sofa centre.*)

BEAUTY. My Dad's a very cruel man, he says I can't go walking
Without my Nurse. It's such a curse—but what's the use of talking?
I wish my Fairy Godmother would come and set me free.

COMPERE. The words are hardly spoken when, defying lock and key,
Through walls of brick twelve inches thick, and doors of stout oak board,
Appears someone we've met before:

(*Enter* MAUD, *with a spindle.*)

MAUD. I am your Auntie Maud.
BEAUTY. You've come to set me free?
MAUD. No no.
COMPERE. Her hopes begin to dwindle.
MAUD. I've brought a present for you.
BEAUTY. Oh, what is it?
MAUD. A spindle.
COMPERE. Alas, the fatal implement the Princess takes in hand.
She does not fear the danger here; she does not understand.
MAUD. Go on dear, feel how sharp it is.
COMPERE. Ah Princess, have a care!
MAUD. Place one small joint upon the point, and press it.
BEAUTY (*pricking herself*). Oh!
MAUD. There, there.
BEAUTY. I feel so faint.
MAUD. Of course you do. Lie down upon this bed.

(BEAUTY *lies on sofa.*)

Revenge at last! She's going fast. She'll very soon be dead.

COMPERE. The wicked fairy dances round with fiendish laughs and jeers,

Then quits the room and mounts her broom, and simply
    disappears. *(Goes out.)*
And now the young Princess's Nurse, attracted by the din,
All out of breath and scared to death, comes quickly
    bursting in.
    (Enter NURSE.*)*

NURSE. Princess, Princess!
COMPERE. In great distress, like some demented thing.
NURSE. My child, my child!
COMPERE. In accents wild, she makes the welkin ring.
NURSE. Oh, art thou feeling faint my dear, or is it indigestion?
Or art thou dead upon thy bed?
COMPERE *(aside).* And that's the Guinea Question!
    *(*NURSE *beckons. Enter* SOLDIER.*)*
The Nurse then calls the Chief of Staff, who calls the
    King again,
    *(*SOLDIER *beckons. Enter* KING, *who beckons.)*
Who calls his spouse. *(Enter* QUEEN.*)* They try to rouse
    their daughter, but in vain.
Then suddenly the Queen espies the spindle on the floor.
QUEEN. Who dares to bring this deadly thing within the palace
    door?
COMPERE. The others all examine it like Customs-house officials;
KING. What's this I see? M.A.U.D.—the Fairy Maud's initials?
COMPERE. So now the horrid truth is out, confirming all their fears:
The Princess gay is doomed to stay asleep a hundred
    years.
QUEEN. If only we could sleep as well!
COMPERE. The Queen in anguish cries.
    (Enter FAIRY 1.*)*
FAIRY 1. No sooner said than done!
COMPERE. And in the leading Fairy flies.
FAIRY 1. Now sit down please. Be quite at ease. You'll soon be
    fast asleep.
And round the wall a forest tall shall constant vigil keep.
    (She looks down at BEAUTY.*)*
So slumber on, fair Beauty, till to wake you with a kiss
A Prince shall come.
SOLDIER *(holding up spindle).* Excuse me, Mum, what shall I do
    with this?
COMPERE. And though the Fairy could have made an answer, that's
    quite certain,

7

Her breath she saves, her wand she waves, and down comes sleep—and curtain.

(They are all asleep, and FAIRY 1 *trips off, as the curtain falls leaving* COMPERE *outside as before.)*

ACT THREE

COMPERE. Now Father Time accelerates to super-sonic pace;
    And past our ears a hundred years have flown without a trace.
    Around the palace, holly trees and prickly brambles sway;
    No mortals dare to venture there—" 'tis haunted," so they say.
    And there, alas, our story ends, for up until tonight,
    Through all these years, no Prince appears, to put our troubles right.
    And whether in the future any Prince will come or no,
    I cannot tell. And so, farewell, and thank you.

CHARLEY *(from back of audience)*.   'arf a mo!

    (CHARLEY *advances to the front, and mounts the stage. He is dressed in "Teddy-boy" style, with cigarette drooping from corner of mouth.)*

COMPERE. But who is this who looks as if he needs a dose of physic,
    With coat so long, and accent strong?

CHARLEY.   I'm Charley Prince of Chiswick.

COMPERE. Thrice welcome Prince, and have you come to break the ancient curse
    Imposed by Maud, and snap the cord of sleep that binds us?

CHARLEY.   Yers.

COMPERE. But can you take a sword in hand, and can you cut a dash,
    And wake the Sleeping Beauty?

CHARLEY.   I dunno, I'll 'ave a bash.

COMPERE. But how to hack through jungle black—that really is a poser—
    And reach the gate?

CHARLEY.   That's easy, mate, I drive me own bull-dozer.

COMPERE *(aside)*.
    This Charley is not quite the sort of Prince they have in books;
    But possibly he may not be as dopey as he looks.

(To CHARLEY.*)*
    Away, then, noble Charley Prince, and break the Fairy's spell.

(CHARLEY *goes out into wings.*)

So off he goes. And I suppose we'd better go as well,
And see just what's been happening within the portico
Where last we saw those sleepers, just a hundred years ago.

(*Curtain up, disclosing the sleepers, still in the same positions, but cobwebs now hang round and above them.*)

How cruel Time has laid his hand upon this little scene!
On all asleep the dust lies deep. I'll show you what I mean:

(COMPERE *blows top of* SOLDIER'S *head and a cloud of dust rises from it.*)

The spider has been busy, too, and spinning finest laces,
Has left the ground and hung them round in most peculiar places.

(COMPERE *removes a cobweb from the* KING'S *face, etc.*)

But now the noble Charley Prince, bull-dozing through the trees,

(*Re-enter* CHARLEY.)

Arrives within the Palace walls, and gasps at what he sees.
Say now, Your Royal Highness, sir—or "Charley" if you'd rather,
What do you think?

CHARLEY (*looking at* KING). Cor strike me pink, the ghost of 'amlet's father!

COMPERE. Come, please approach as tenderly and softly as you may,
And gently plant a loving kiss on Beauty's lips.

CHARLEY (*moving up behind* BEAUTY'S *couch*).   O.K.

COMPERE. Now are you ready, noble Prince?

CHARLEY.   I've got me lips all pursed.

COMPERE. If you don't mind, it might be kind to take your fag out first.

(CHARLEY *removes cigarette.*)

In silence let us gaze upon this scene of purest bliss,
As Charley P., on bended knee, wakes Beauty with a kiss.

(CHARLEY *kisses* BEAUTY. *All wake and stretch.* BEAUTY *does not see* CHARLEY *who is behind her as she sits up*).

KING (*yawning*). Ah, what's the time?

SOLDIER.   Your Majesty, my watch has stopped at five.

KING.   It feels so late. Oh, what a state!

QUEEN.	Come husband, look alive; It's Friday, I must get some fish, and you must pay the wages.
KING.	I feel so stiff, it's just as if I'd been asleep for ages.
BEAUTY.	Oh where—?—
NURSE.	Don't interrupt, my dear, just beg your Daddy's pardon. And now you know, it's time to go for walkies in the garden; So upsy-daisy.
BEAUTY *(looking round)*.	Go away. Where is he? Where's my Prince? That best of men who kissed me then?
CHARLEY.	I've been 'ere ever since.
BEAUTY.	I mean the Prince who rescued me.
CHARLEY.	That's right.
BEAUTY.	It wasn't *you?*
CHARLEY.	It *was*, you know.
BEAUTY.	Oh say not so! It simply can't be true.
COMPERE.	Princess, the young man speaks the truth. It happened as he said. Now will you take him for your mate, and will you with him wed?
BEAUTY.	That little pest? If that's the best this century can show, Then pass me up the spindle, I'll go back to sleep.

(Enter a real PRINCE, dressed in traditional princely style.)

PRINCE.	No, no!
COMPERE.	Now just a minute, first of all, before we all get dizzy, Please tell us who you are.
PRINCE.	I am a Royal Prince.
CHARLEY.	Oh, is he?
PRINCE.	Your Highness, I am here at last. I'm sorry I was late Some silly pig had parked a big bull-dozer in the gate. I got my men to push it in the castle moat, and so My coach and four are at the door. Come Princess, shall we go?
BEAUTY.	Most gladly.
CHARLEY.	I say, wait a bit!
COMPERE.	But Charley pleads in vain. The King and Queen their blessing give, and tripping in again,

(Enter the FAIRIES, including MAUD.)
The Fairies all, both short and tall, bring presents for the Bride;
Except old Maud, who's quite ignored.

MAUD. Once more I am defied!
On one condition only, the Princess can go free—
And that is if the Prince who kissed her lips shall marry me!
(She opens her arms towards the PRINCE.)

PRINCE. Agreed. }
BEAUTY. Agreed. } *(They push CHARLEY into MAUD'S arms.)*

CHARLEY. 'ere, wait a bit!

COMPERE. But there's no time to parley;
So Beauty gets a proper Prince, and Maud a proper Charley.

(The Curtains close, then immediately open again, and the players come forward in couples to make their bows to the audience and then go into the wings or walk down through the hall. The PRINCE and BEAUTY come first, and then the KING and QUEEN, and the SOLDIER and NURSE. The FAIRIES follow in pairs, the last pair—or odd one—holds out a hand to the COMPERE who accompanies them, with a wink at the audience. CHARLEY and MAUD are left alone. Suddenly MAUD throws off her enveloping black cloak, revealing sweater and slacks, or similar clothes of gaudy pattern, flashy jewellery, etc., so that she looks exactly the female counterpart to CHARLEY. They embrace and march off together, arm in arm.

THE END

PRODUCTION NOTE

This is intended to be a complete "rag" and should be played as such—and the "hammier" the better. No attempt should be made at realism, but of course it is important for the players to speak the exact lines allotted to them, no more and no less; otherwise the impact of the atrocious verse will be lost.

Setting can be as simple or elaborate as you like. The only essential pieces of furniture are a sofa or couch (or three chairs in a row!) for BEAUTY to lie on, and a cot. (Act One only.)

Costumes can easily be concocted from wardrobe, dressing-up box and rag-bag. The royal family should have cardboard crowns, and the SOLDIER something that looks like uniform. CHARLEY and MAUD are described in the text.

Silver dishes can be tin plates or cardboard plates painted silver. An old chair leg makes an admirable spindle. Cobwebs can be made out of thick string, or wire, or even painted on pieces of paper and pinned to the walls. The effect of blowing dust from the SOLDIER'S head can be obtained by depositing a small heap of powder on his head before the curtain rises on Act Three.

The COMPERE can best be described as a cross between a Circus Ringmaster and a B.B.C. Announcer—with a dash of the Music Hall Chairman thrown in.

Don't worry if you have not enough men or women to make a balanced cast, nobody will mind. Good luck to all who try it!

RICHARD TYDEMAN.

Iron-Hot Strikers

An All-Women Minidrama

Richard Tydeman

A SAMUEL FRENCH ACTING EDITION

SAMUELFRENCH-LONDON.CO.UK
SAMUELFRENCH.COM

A Minidrama for a dozen or more women—and the more the merrier. A few medium-sized parts, a lot of very small parts, and no large ones. Can be performed on a stage or in arena—or, of course, in a canteen.

CHARACTERS
in order of their appearance

MAVIS
NOREEN } *canteen workers*
YOUNG EFF
MISS SPINKS, *a trade union official*
MISS CRANE, *a shop steward*
GLADYS
HATTIE
VERA } *laundry workers*
DORIS
FRANCES
JANEY, *a bride*
MRS. WAKEFIELD, *the manageress*

also other laundry workers and bridesmaids
SCENE: The canteen of a laundry

IRON-HOT STRIKERS

Enter MAVIS *and* NOREEN *carrying trays or wheeling a trolley. They start laying tables for lunch.*

MAVIS (*as they enter*). So I said to him, I said, if that's how you want it to be, Sparkie, then that's how it had better be.

NOREEN. And was it?

MAVIS. Was it what?—How he wanted it, or How it turned out?

NOREEN. Well, either.

MAVIS. No. Because you see Sparkie knows I didn't mean it and I knew he knew. I always know what Sparkie knows, you know.

NOREEN (*doubtfully*). Oh.

MAVIS. Well, wouldn't you?

NOREEN. I dunno. I suppose so. I say, his name isn't really Sparkie, is it?

MAVIS. No, only I always call him that, ever since one day when he lost his voice shouting at an echo.

NOREEN (*doubtfully*). Oh.

MAVIS. Where's Young Eff with those knives. Young Eff!

EFF (*appearing with tray*). Coming.

(YOUNG EFF *is not so very young, but simple and untidy and slow.*)

MAVIS. About time, too. Here's Noreen and me working our fingers to the bone. You want to get up a bit earlier in the morning.

EFF. I got up at seven.

MAVIS. Seven! Why, Noreen and me had done half a day's work by that time.

EFF. You must have got up in the middle of the night, then.

MAVIS. That's right. Now hurry up and lay them knives round.

NOREEN. What's the time?

MAVIS. Nearly twelve.

NOREEN. I hope Janey will come in here before she goes off to church.

MAVIS. She'd better! She promised us a look at the bridesmaids, too.

NOREEN. I've never been a bridesmaid, have you, Mavis?

MAVIS. Hundreds of times.

EFF. Mavis.

MAVIS. Well?

EFF. If you did half a day's work before seven, you must have got up before I went to sleep.

MAVIS. That would take some doing. I've never seen you when you *wasn't* asleep. Now get a move on.

(EFF *starts laying knives.*)
NOREEN. What are they having today?
MAVIS. Shepherd's pie of course. It's Wednesday, isn't it?
NOREEN. Oh yes, that's right.
MAVIS. They'd have it every day if I had my way. Easiest dinner in the world, shepherd's pie. Nothing to carve up, no extra vegetable dishes, just one good dollop on each plate and they've got the lot.
EFF. Except the gravy.
MAVIS. Well, wonders never cease! She's not only alive, but awake and listening! Yes, of course, the gravy's your job, isn't it?
EFF. Mavis.
MAVIS. Well?
EFF. Shepherd's pie is that stuff you eat with a fork, isn't it?
MAVIS. There's a bright girl for you! Yes, Young Eff, you take the fork in the right hand, (*Demonstrating.*) pick up a mouthful from the plate and convey it to the ruby lips, thus. (EFF *stares at her.*) So what?
EFF. I was wondering why they needed all these knives.
MAVIS. Didn't your mother never learn you nothing? The way people eat and the way we lay their tables is two entirely different things.
EFF. Why?
MAVIS. Never mind why. You get on and do it, and do it proper. (*Turning to* NOREEN.) What would you do with her, Noreen, eh?
NOREEN. I admire your patience, Mavis, I do indeed.
MAVIS. Patience! On a monument, that's where I ought to be, on a monument. Come on.
    (*Exeunt* MAVIS *and* NOREEN. EFF *continues to lay tables. Enter, from another direction,* MISS SPINKS.)
SPINKS. Good morning. (EFF *takes no notice.*) Good morning. (EFF *still takes no notice, so* SPINKS *stands right in front of her and speaks loudly.*) Good morning.
EFF (*after looking over her shoulder to make sure that* SPINKS *is really speaking to her and not to someone behind her*). Hullo.
SPINKS. You are Mrs. Mavis Manders?
EFF. No. I'm Young Eff.
SPINKS. Is Mrs. Manders here?
EFF. In there.
SPINKS. Can I see her?
EFF. If she isn't too tired.
SPINKS. Tired?
EFF. She's been up all night. Did half a day's work before seven o'clock this morning.

SPINKS. Good gracious! Well, please tell her that I represent the Laundering, Pressing and Catering Trades Union and I would like to speak to her. Spinks is the name.
EFF (*suddenly shaking hands with her*). How do you do?
SPINKS (*surprised*). Oh, yes, of course. How do you do? Now perhaps you will kindly tell Mrs. Manders that I am here. (*Sits at an unlaid table.*)
EFF. All right. (*She starts to go, then picks up a knife, returns to* SPINKS *who shrinks back in alarm.* EFF *lays knife on* SPINKS' *table.*) You'll want a knife.
SPINKS. Whatever for?
EFF. For not eating your shepherd's pie with. (*Exit.*)
(*Enter from another direction* MISS CRANE, *shop steward.*)
CRANE. Ah, there you are, Miss Spinks.
SPINKS. Well?
CRANE. It's no good. They are quite determined. Oh yes, I know just what you are going to say: if they strike, the Union will not support them.
SPINKS. It isn't that the Union *will* not support them—it *cannot* support them. I have already explained that.
CRANE. I don't think you realize the feeling there is in this laundry, Miss Spinks. Whenever one of our girls has got married, the others have *always* been allowed time off to go and watch. It's a sort of tradition.
SPINKS. The Union has its rules, Miss Crane, and in those rules there is nothing about weddings. No doubt there ought to be, in view of the popularity of such ceremonies, but there isn't.
CRANE. Look—all the girls want is an hour off, to go round the corner and watch Janey come out of church. That's all. Just one hour.
SPINKS. For which the firm is paying an average of—shall we say?—five shillings a head. How many girls want to go?
CRANE. About forty.
SPINKS. So the firm is to pay ten pounds for an hour in which no work is done.
CRANE. They could call it a wedding present.
SPINKS. In my experience wedding presents are usually given to the bride, not to the spectators outside the church. No, it's no good, Miss Crane. I have had a long conversation with the Manageress.
CRANE. I know just what you are going to say—she was adamant.
SPINKS. She was indeed.
CRANE. New brooms usually are. We never had any trouble when Mr. Wakefield was here himself, but ever since he went off to America and left his wife in charge—well, words fail me!

IRON-HOT STRIKERS

(*Re-enter* MAVIS.)

MAVIS. Oh, good morning.

CRANE. Ah, here is Mrs. Manders, the head of our catering department. Mavis, this is Miss Spinks, of the Union.

MAVIS. Pleased to meet you, I'm sure.

SPINKS. Mrs. Manders, I wonder if we could have a little chat somewhere?

MAVIS. You can come into my office—(*They start to go.*)—if you like to call it an office—it's really a corner of the kitchen screened off with hardboard where I keep the books and things. I really ought to have something better than that and I shall be glad if you could do something about . . .

(*They have all gone. Immediately the noise of an approaching crowd is heard from the other direction and there enter a number of laundry workers carrying placards with "Strike Now", "We Want Weddings" etc. They form a group round the leader,* GLADYS, *who mounts on a chair. They make a lot of noise.*)

GLADYS. All right. Quiet, please. Quiet. (*The noise continues.*) Oh, listen a minute. (*Amid a chorus of "shush" etc., the noise dies down.*) That's better. Now you all know what this meeting is about. We have been refused permission to go and see Janey come out of church. (*Angry agreement.*) It has been the custom in this laundry to allow one hour off for a wedding, ever since I can remember. We must demand our rights!

ALL. Hear, hear! (*Etc.*)

GLADYS. Now we have tried to bring in the Union on our side, but I'm afraid Miss Spinks has been got at by Mrs. Wakefield. (*Chorus of "Boo" etc.*) Therefore the strike, if there is a strike, will have to be "unofficial", and we shall have to have one hundred per cent agreement to make it effective. Before I put it to the vote, are there any questions?

HATTIE (*nervously*). Could I ask . . .

GLADYS. Yes, Hattie, what is it?

HATTIE. Will the new vicar be taking the service?

GLADYS. What's that got to do with it?

HATTIE (*sighing*). Oh, he's such a lovely man.

SEVERAL VOICES. Shut up, Hattie. (*Etc.*)

HATTIE. Well, he *is*. I wouldn't strike over Janey, but I would if it meant not seeing the new vicar.

GLADYS. Then you'd better strike, because if you don't, you won't see anybody.

HATTIE. Archibald Tomlinson his name is. I think it suits him.

(*The others sit on* HATTIE *either metaphorically or physically, or both.*)

GLADYS. Now, any more questions?

VERA. Suppose Mrs. Wakefield gives us the sack.

GLADYS. She won't do that. She knows perfectly well that she would never be able to replace us.

DORIS. What about the customers?

GLADYS. Customers? Why should we worry about them? We're human beings, aren't we? We have our rights. Now, I'm going to put this to the vote straight away. Those in favour of immediate strike action . . .

(*Enter* FRANCES. *If necessary she could already be one of the crowd on stage who has moved towards exit as if to look off.*)

FRANCES. She's coming!

(*Consternation. Placards are hidden,* GLADYS *jumps down. All try and get behind and push her forward, obviously expecting the* MANAGERESS.)

What's the matter? Don't you want to see her?

GLADYS. Well—of course—we are always pleased to see Mrs. Wakefield.

FRANCES. It's not Mrs. Wakefield, silly, it's Janey.

(*Enter* JANEY *in wedding dress, with one or more bridesmaids. Consternation changes to excitement and pleasure as all crowd round her.*)

JANEY. I couldn't find you. What are you all doing in the canteen?

VERA (*after an awkward silence*). We're having an extra tea break before we come down to the church.

JANEY. Oh, you *are* coming then. I'm so glad. Somebody downstairs said you wouldn't be able to get off.

GLADYS (*grimly*). We're going to get off all right.

JANEY. Well, what do you think of the dresses?

(*All admire dresses of bride and bridesmaids, ad lib., commenting on the design, material, workmanship, etc. Then* JANEY *catches sight of* HATTIE.)

Oh, Hattie, there was a message downstairs from the vicar.

HATTIE. For me? A message for me? From him? Oh! (*She has to be helped to a chair.*) Tell me.

JANEY. He wants to know what has happened to the surplices.

HATTIE (*jumping up*). The surplices? They should be at the church. The ones for the choir were ready yesterday and I ironed Mr. Tomlinson's myself, first thing this morning. I wrapped it in tissue paper and sprinkled a few drops of my perfume on it just for luck. (*Distracted.*) They should have gone. I'll go and see. If they are still there I will take them myself, this minute. (*Exit.*)

JANEY. Poor Hattie.
DORIS. Poor vicar. Hattie's perfume cost one and six for a large bottle.
> (*Re-enter* MAVIS, *followed by* SPINKS *and* CRANE, NOREEN *and* YOUNG EFF.)

MAVIS. Now, what's going on out here, eh? Why, it's Janey!
> (NOREEN *and* EFF *come to greet* JANEY.)

SPINKS. So this is the cause of all the trouble.
JANEY. Trouble?
CRANE (*whispering to* SPINKS). We haven't told her about the strike. We don't want to spoil her day.
JANEY. What trouble have I caused?
SPINKS. Oh, nothing, my dear. Just a metaphorical expression.
NOREEN. Like saying, "may all your troubles be little ones".
EFF. Yes, Janey's troubles always were little ones, weren't they?
MAVIS. You keep quiet, Young Eff. Well, Janey, we all hope you will be very, very happy.
JANEY. I'm sure I shall. Thank you all for your good wishes and for the lovely presents and things. And now we must run or we shall be late. See you all outside the church. (*To* BRIDESMAIDS.) Come on, girls.
> (*Amid a chorus of "Good luck" etc.*, JANEY *and bridesmaids go off. There is silence, then all sigh.*)

CRANE (*to* SPINKS). Well, you see how it is.
SPINKS (*sighing*). Yes, I know what you mean.
CRANE. I think we shall have to strike.
SPINKS. I think you will.
GLADYS. You hear that girls? The strike is on!
> (*All cheer and raise placards again.*)

Come on then.
> (*But as they turn to go, a forbidding figure stands in their way. It is* MRS. WAKEFIELD.)

MRS. WAKEFIELD. Good morning.
ALL (*sheepishly*). Good morning, Mrs. Wakefield.
MRS. WAKEFIELD. It's a bit early for lunch, isn't it?
GLADYS. We're going—
CRANE. We've decided—
SPINKS. I think I ought to tell you—
MRS. WAKEFIELD. I do not wish to know *why* you are here, but I am glad of the opportunity of addressing you all together. I am making an important change in this laundry which will affect many of you. By introducing new machinery I propose to cut down the number

of staff by fifty per cent. I shall naturally keep on the employees who are the most loyal and hard-working.

SPINKS. I think I should have had notice of this.

MRS. WAKEFIELD. "Notice" is perhaps not a very tactful word to use, Miss Spinks, because "Notice" is what I shall have to give to those who are disloyal or disobedient. Is that clearly understood?

ALL (*unwillingly*). Yes, Mrs. Wakefield.

(*Re-enter* HATTIE *with two parcels—a large one wrapped in brown paper and string, and a small one in white paper tied with coloured ribbon.*)

HATTIE. Just going. I do hope I am in time. Those silly people in the dispatch department say they are on str— (*Sees* MRS. WAKEFIELD.) Oh!

MRS. WAKEFIELD. Wedding presents, Harriet?

HATTIE. No, no, Mrs. Wakefield, these are the surplices for the church. The choir robes are in this parcel, and the other one is for the Reverend Archibald Tomlinson, our beloved vicar.

MRS. WAKEFIELD. I see. (*Taking them from her.*) Well, you can safely leave them to me and I will see they are delivered—as soon as everyone is back at work. Good morning. (*Exit.*)

(*There is a stunned silence and then* HATTIE *springs to life wailing as she runs after her.*)

HATTIE. Oh, no, Mrs. Wakefield, he must have it now. His spare one has a hole in the sleeve where he tore it on a gravestone and it hasn't been mended yet, so it is most important— (*She has gone.*)

CRANE. Now what do we do?

GLADYS. We mustn't give in. Whatever happens, the strike must go on. (*Some approve of this but others don't.*)

DORIS. I vote we go back to work.

VERA. Hear, hear. We don't want to lose our jobs.

GLADYS. Blacklegs!

CRANE. Now, let us be calm. As shop steward I beg you to consider this matter from every angle. What exactly have we got on our plate?

EFF. Shepherd's pie. One good dollop each and—

MAVIS. That's enough, Young Eff.

EFF. Not for me it isn't, I like two good dollops.

NOREEN. Here, Eff, go and make us all a nice cup of tea.

(*Chorus of "Hear, Hear", "Good idea", etc.*)

EFF. You're trying to get rid of me, aren't you? (NOREEN *and* MAVIS *glare at her.*) Oh, all right. (*Moving away.*) Soppy lot! (*Exit.*)

CRANE. Now, going back to what I was saying.

SPINKS (*who has been studying a small book*). May I speak please, Miss Crane?

CRANE. Well...

GLADYS. No, don't let her. She isn't on our side.

SPINKS. But I am. I have been looking up my book of rules, and I believe that the situation is now completely altered. I could not advise you to strike before, but now Mrs. Wakefield has threatened you with dismissal and that is intimidation; the Union will not stand for intimidation.

(*Cheers and "Good old* SPINKS" *etc.*)

CRANE. So the strike can be official now.

SPINKS. Yes, indeed.

CRANE. Do you all agree? (*All indicate agreement.*) Right. A strike it is. (*Re-enter* EFF. *She advances to* C. *and sits.*)

NOREEN. Now then, Young Eff, what's this? Where's that cup of tea?

EFF. Can't make no tea.

NOREEN. Why not?

EFF. I'm on strike. (*Noisy disapproval.*)

MAVIS. The strike's got nothing to do with the kitchen staff.

EFF. Oh, yes, it has. I've come out in sympathy.

MAVIS. Sympathy! (*They all talk at once and argue over this. Re-enter* HATTIE, *dishevelled and carrying the white parcel tenderly.*)

HATTIE. I rescued it.

GLADYS. Hattie!

HATTIE. I have fought a righteous battle and recovered holy things from the hands of the ungodly. (*They all stare at her.*) Oh, by the way, Mr. Wakefield is home from America. (*Pleased exclamations.*) He has just arrived and to celebrate his return he says we can all have the rest of the day off.

(*Loud cheers.*)

CRANE. But this is wonderful. We shan't need to strike after all.

SPINKS. A very happy solution.

GLADYS. A pity, but still it was worth it.

NOREEN. Come on then, what are we waiting for? Let's get down to the church. We might even see her go in.

(*All agree cheerfully, abandon placards and turn to go. As they do so,* JANEY *and bridesmaids run on in tears.*)

MAVIS. Good gracious, Janey, what's the matter?

JANEY. It's off.

MAVIS. What's off?

JANEY. The wedding. Oh, I'm so miserable. (*Sympathetic murmurs.*) And it's all your fault!

GLADYS. *Our* fault!
JANEY. Where are those surplices?
HATTIE. Oh, well, they're here, but I'm just going.
JANEY. Too late. The vicar's gone home.
HATTIE. He's not hurt is he?
JANEY. No.
HATTIE. Or ill? He's not ill?
JANEY. No, no, he's—he's—
ALL. Well?
JANEY (*wailing*). He's gone on strike!
  CURTAIN, BLACKOUT, OR GENERAL QUICK EXIT

PRODUCTION NOTES

Iron-Hot Strikers can be performed on any stage or platform, but it would probably be more effective in a larger space, and would lend itself to "in-the-round" production where more tables and chairs could be used and the atmosphere of the canteen suggested. Stage directions in the text have been kept to a bare minimum to give the producer a free hand according to the space available.

A large crowd of laundry workers is not essential but would obviously be more effective. If you are lucky enough to have a crowd, don't leave them as an indeterminate herd, but encourage each to be an individual, reacting in her own particular way to everything that is said or done.

Costumes will present no difficulty. The canteen workers should have some kind of uniform but the laundry workers, being on the verge of a strike, could quite easily have discarded their uniforms before entering. I would not presume to suggest what sort of dresses the bride and bridesmaids should wear!

Keep a good pace going, but do wait for laughs—and let's hope that the audience doesn't go on strike before the end of the performance!

              RICHARD TYDEMAN

Piccalilli Circus

A Pickled Minidrama of the Big Top

Richard Tydeman

A Samuel French Acting Edition

SAMUELFRENCH-LONDON.CO.UK
SAMUELFRENCH.COM

PICCALILLI CIRCUS

After suitable circus music, the COMPERE *appears in front of curtains, dressed as a ringmaster and carrying a copy of the script.*

COMPERE. Your Graces, My Lords, Ladies and Gentlemen!
Whether you've paid two bob or one pound ten,
We welcome you, and hope you will enjoy
Our story of a circus girl and boy;
This strange compound of tragedy and mirth—
A peep behind the Greatest Show on Earth.
But, oh my friends, we are not here to bring
The spangles and the glitter of the ring.
Instead the artistes, in a tent below,
Are resting after finishing their show.

(Curtain rises, and COMPERE *moves to left of proscenium arch.* D.R., FAY, SPIKE *and* LEO *are sitting on wooden boxes playing cards.* U.L., JACK *the strong man is practising lifting what appears to be a very heavy weight.)*

No glamour here, far from the limelight's flame.
Observe their concentration on the game.

FAY. It is your turn.

COMPERE. The Tight Rope Walker cries,
Looking the Lion Tamer in the eyes.
Beneath that black moustache with waxen tips,
The Lion Tamer bites his trembling lips.
Now the Knife Thrower draws a glittering blade:

SPIKE. Your turn.

COMPERE. His voice demands to be obeyed.

LEO. My turn? All right. Please put away your knife.
Have you got Mrs. Bones the Butcher's Wife?

SPIKE. Ha ha! Have I got Mrs. Bones? Why, no sir!
I'll trouble you for Mr. Grits the Grocer.

*(*LEO *hands him a card and the game continues silently.)*

COMPERE. Now, all this time the Strong Man activates
His mighty muscles, lifting heavy weights.
No time has he for frivolous enjoyment,
Engaged in such a strenuous employment.

(Enter CLARICE, *the Equestrienne. She stands* C., *watching* JACK *with folded arms.)*

But who is this, so statuesque and stately,
Who enters all so silent and sedately?
The best that ever stood on horse's back—
Clarice, champion circus rider.

CLARICE (*loudly*).   Jack!
> (JACK *drops the weight with a bang and hops round holding his toe.*)

You've got to stop them—stop them! Do you hear?
Keep still. I'm talking to you.

JACK (*standing up straight*).   Yes, my dear.

CLARICE. I caught them kissing—kissing, if you please,
Between the Tigers and the Chimpanzees!
Well, don't just stand there motionless, you dunce.

JACK. Ah yes, my dear, I'll see to it at once.
> (*He limps off.* CLARICE *easily picks up his heavy weight with one hand and follows him off.*)

FAY. You must have Master Potts the Painter's Son;
Also the Baker's Lady, Mrs. Bunn.
> (CAPP, *the Clown, enters. He gives an exaggerated impression of the "broken heart behind the smiling face".*)

CAPP. Hullo, hullo, and here we are again.
Alas, alas, my heart is filled with pain.
The people laugh to see me in the ring;
"On with the motley" and that sort of thing.
Ah me! My life is like an empty bubble.

COMPERE. Poor fellow. Why, what seems to be the trouble?

CAPP. My only daughter, the ungrateful brat,
Has gone and fallen for an acrobat.

COMPERE. Son of the Strong Man and the Bare-back Rider—
Young Rolio?

CAPP.   The same. A rank outsider!

COMPERE. But what's so serious—

CAPP.   I caught a glimpse
Out there between the Tigers and the Chimps.
> (*He shudders and turns away with a tragic gesture.*)

COMPERE (*to audience*). The situation's this: Young Rolio
Is of the Monti family you know.
While this poor Clown—you will have guessed perhaps,
Is of the rival family of Capps.
Between the Capps and Montis there's a feud
Of bitter hatred, constantly renewed.

CAPP. The most expensive luxuries I've bought her!

FAY. And now I'll have Miss Tape, the Tailor's Daughter.
> (*Enter* JUNE, *young and beautiful.*)

JUNE. Oh Daddy dear.

CAPP.   My June! What have you done?

JUNE. Why, nothing. We were only having fun.
CAPP. All further fun I utterly forbid.
  Go to your mother.
JUNE (*crying*).   Oh! (*Goes out.*)
SPIKE.   Poor little kid.
CAPP (*to* SPIKE). You spoke sir?
SPIKE (*ignoring him*).   I'll have Mr. Bung the Brewer.
CAPP. This insolence is more than I'll endure.
  You are for Monti?
SPIKE.   Go and call the banns.
  I say, a plague on both your caravans!
CAPP. Monti shall die!
COMPERE.   Look out then. Here he comes.
        (*Enter* CLARICE *and* JACK, *with* ROLIO *their son between them.*)
CLARICE. Thou treacherous Capp, at thee we bite our thumbs.
        (CLARICE *and* JACK *bite their thumbs.*)
ROLIO. Nay, father, mother, for I love her true.
  My June is everything—
CLARICE *and* JACK (*pushing him to his knees*). Be quiet, you.
CAPP. This is too much. My anger now beware!
CLARICE. Jack Monti, show him you're the master.
JACK (*making a long nose at* CAPP, *from behind* CLARICE). There!
        (*Pandemonium, all shouting at each other.* FAY *and* LEO *join in, eventually* FAY *leads* CAPP *off one way while* LEO *takes the Monti family off the other. Only* SPIKE *remains seated, unmoved, with cards still in his hand.*)
SPIKE. When merry circus people take their ease,
  They love a game of Happy Families.
        (CURTAIN *falls, leaving* COMPERE *outside.*)
COMPERE. 'Tis as I said. The glamour and the spangles
  Are bright enough if seen from certain angles;
  But underneath a glittering façade
  The circus artiste's lot is mighty hard.
  They work together, putting on the show;
  They smile together as we cry, "Bravo";
  With arms entwined they greet our wild applause.
  But if you could but see beyond closed doors—
  For instance, in the caravan of Capp
  There's shortly going to be a fearful scrap;
  And may the best man win. Amen. So be it.
  I've talked for long enough. Let's go and see it.
        (*Curtain rises. The Capp caravan, purely imaginary or indicated by scenery, occupies the* C. *and* R. *of the stage. Only the living-room is on the stage; the bedrooms are off* R. *A small table and at least two chairs with cushions are placed slightly* R. *of* C. *Entrance to the caravan is imagined as being* L.C. *Players entering or leaving it should open and*

close imaginary door. MONA, *the Clown's wife, is in the caravan talking to* JUNE.)
There's Mrs. Capp, she's married to the Clown.
MONA. Oh daughter June, you've let your father down.
Young Rolio's a Monti. Don't you think
That such a union would cause a stink?
JUNE. Rolio, Rolio, why, what's in a name?
MONA. By any other it would smell the same.
            (JUNE *weeps*.)
There, there.
COMPERE.   But comfort comes a trifle late,
For now there enters, like avenging Fate,
The furious Capp.
            (*Enter* CAPP, L.)
CAPP.   Abused! Insulted! Mocked!
He bit his thumbs—a snook at me he cocked!
I'll have his blood.
MONA.   June dear, you'd better hide.
JUNE. Oh Mum, I knew that you'd be on my side.
    (JUNE *goes off* R. CAPP *moves through imaginary door into caravan*.)
CAPP. Where is she?
MONA.   Who?
CAPP.   That stupid little wench.
COMPERE. Bravely she strives her husband's wrath to quench.
    She sits him down.
MONA (*taking cushion from other chair*). This cushion would be better.
COMPERE. But see, behind the cushion is—a letter!
CAPP (*seeing it*). What letter's that?
MONA (*trying to cover up*). Oh, some old tradesman's bill.
CAPP (*snatching it*). A Monti's hand! Alas, this likes me ill.
COMPERE. With trembling fingers he extracts the note
    Which to his daughter Rolio had wrote.
    (I think that last word really should be "written".
    Our author's chewed off more than he has bitten.)
CAPP (*reading*). "Tonight at midnight to thy balcony
    Thy Rolio shall climb. Oh fly with me."
    Perfidious spider! Shall thy net enmesh her?
MONA. Oh husband, pray remember your blood pressure.
COMPERE. With soothing words the lady bids him rest.
MONA. I'm sure that all will turn out for the best.
COMPERE. But now a plan there forms his brain within.
    Upon his face appears a cunning grin.
CAPP. Please make the tea.
COMPERE (*as* MONA *goes off* R.). She hastens to obey;
    And soon as she is safely on her way

A pen he takes, and in his daughter's writing
Constructs an answer, tender and inviting:
CAPP (*as he writes*). "At midnight I will fly with thee, my honey.
   P.S. Be sure to bring a lot of money."
COMPERE. The note is sealed; to Rolio addressed.
CAPP. Now will I drive this cuckoo from my nest.
   When he tonight comes serenading June,
   My stick shall make him sing another tune.
       (*Taking note, he leaves caravan, closing imaginary door quietly, and goes off* L.)
COMPERE. Light-hearted now, and on his lips a whistle,
   He disappears to plant his false epistle.
   June hears him go and cautiously emerges,
       (JUNE *enters and sees the letter from* ROLIO.)
   But consternation in her bosom surges.
JUNE. He's seen it! Now there'll be the deuce to pay.
   I must warn Rolio without delay.
COMPERE. And leaving not a moment for reflection,
   She exits in the opposite direction.
       (JUNE *leaves caravan by imaginary door, and then goes off* D.R. MONA *re-enters* U.R., *with tea*.)
MONA. Tea's made. (*Looking round.*) He's gone!—without a "where"
                                                           or "when".
   Oh, isn't that just typical of men!
       (CURTAIN *falls, leaving* COMPERE *outside*.)
COMPERE. The action of our story now has shifted;
   And I'm not telepathically gifted,
   So we'll shift with it, past the Polar Bears,
   Around the Elephants and up the stairs
   To Monti's caravan which is, you know,
   The home of Clarice, Jack and Rolio.
   All caravans are bound to look the same
   No matter what the occupier's name.
   So just to make such difference as we may,
   We've turned the Montis' round the other way.
       (CURTAIN *up. Table and chairs are now slightly* L. *of* C., *bedrooms are off* L., *and imaginary door is* R.C. *As curtain rises*, CLARICE, ROLIO *and* JACK *enter* R., *and go through imaginary door into caravan*.)
JACK. He threatened us.
CLARICE.   If you were half a man
   You'd fight that fellow Capp.
JACK.   I can't.
CLARICE.   You can.
   (*To* ROLIO). And as for you, you pipsqueak, pimple, pup!
   What do you say?
ROLIO.   I only want—

CLARICE.   Shut up!
COMPERE. So time goes by in pleasant conversation.
  Such harmony requires no explanation.
  I'm sure your family is just as kind
  To one another? (*Peers hard at audience.*) Oh well, never mind.
                (CAPP *enters stealthily* D.R.)
  What's this? 'Tis Capp the Clown with stealthy tread.
CLARICE. Now Rolio, you'd better go to bed.
ROLIO. To bed, mamma?
JACK.   I think I'd do it, son.
  You know your mother never speaks in fun.
COMPERE. With dragging steps the boy departs.
ROLIO (*moving slowly* L.).   All right.
COMPERE. And turns to give his final word:
ROLIO (*turns, takes breath, then changes his mind*). Good night.
    (*Exit* ROLIO L. CAPP *creeps, stooping, along front of stage,
  counting imaginary windows.*)
COMPERE. Now Capp approaches, hoping he can throw
  His letter to be found by Rolio.
  He counts the windows, for he knows, you see,
  The single room is window number three.
  But as this caravan's the wrong way round,
        (CAPP *throws letter which lands near* CLARICE.)
  His letter simply falls upon the ground
  Right at the feet of Clarice.
                (*Exit* CAPP L.)
JACK (*staring at the letter*). Look, my dear,
  A note.
CLARICE (*holding out her hand*). Well, pick it up and pass it here.
        (JACK *picks up letter and hands it to her.*)
COMPERE. The lady opens up the *billet doux*;
  At arm's length holds it out and reads it through,
  Then hands it back. Her dainty fingers dusting,
  She gives her verdict in one word:
CLARICE.   Disgusting!
JACK. What shall we do?
CLARICE.   Now Rolio's in bed,
  The answer's easy: I shall go instead.
    (JUNE *enters* U.R., *crosses stealthily and goes off* L.)
  Go, fetch me your old overcoat and slacks.
  Instead of smacking kisses, she'll get smacks!
         (CURTAIN *falls, leaving* COMPERE *outside.*)
COMPERE. Now did you notice, as that scene was ending,
  Young June, our heroine, her way was wending
  Around the Monti caravan by night?
  She knows where Rolio's window is all right!

No time she's wasting in procrastination.
> (*Enter, in front of curtain,* FAY, LEO *and* SPIKE. *They stand in a row with folded arms.*)

Hullo, now what's this little deputation?
LEO.   It isn't fair.
FAY.   It's monstrous.
SPIKE.   We're on strike.
COMPERE.   Why, what's the matter? Something you don't like?
SPIKE.   This minidrama's very nearly done,
  And we've made no appearance since scene one.
LEO.   The author said we could have twelve lines each,
  And up till now I've only had one speech.
FAY.   I think we're justified in being heated,
  We have been most abominably treated.
COMPERE.   I see your point. No doubt somebody slipped;
  But I can't help—we must stick to the script.
FAY.   Couldn't we just—oh no, perhaps we couldn't.
LEO.   Wouldn't it do if—no, you're right, it wouldn't.
SPIKE.   It isn't only lines we want. In fact
  We'd be content to do our circus act.
> (FAY *and* LEO *nod.*)

COMPERE.   All right. I'll give you, while they change the scene,
  One minute each to show us what you mean.
  You first. (*He turns to* FAY.)
FAY.   I have no tight rope here you know;
  But if I had, I'd walk upon it, so.
> (*She gives dumb-show imitation of a tight rope act.*)

COMPERE.   Bravo! That was an act to keep one's eye on.
  (*To* LEO.) And now please show us how you tame a lion.
LEO.   I have no lion here. But still, at least,
  You can perhaps imagine such a beast.
> (*Gives imitation of training a lion to lie down, stand up, jump through hoop, etc.*)

COMPERE.   That's splendid. (*To* SPIKE.) Now, I think you throw the knife?
SPIKE.   These twenty blades I circle round my wife.
> (*He throws twenty imaginary knives off stage. Someone in the wings makes suitable noises each time.*)

COMPERE.   You're happy?
SPIKE.   Thank you very much indeed.
  We'll call the strike off. Let the play proceed.
> (FAY, LEO *and* SPIKE *go off.*)

COMPERE.   Well, after that unusual demonstration,
  I trust I can return to my narration.
  Our final scene: Capp's caravan we see,

(CURTAIN *rises. We are back at* CAPP'S *caravan. It is dark.*
CAPP *sits enveloped in a cloak.*)
Waiting the stroke of midnight patiently,
Disguised as June, this clumsiest of clowns
Sitting; while in her husband's reach-me-downs,
Clarice arrives disguised as Rolio,
With Jack, her strong and silent man in tow.
  (*Enter* L., CLARICE *in overcoat and slacks.* JACK *follows her, carrying an electric torch.*)
CLARICE. This is the place. Be careful what you're at.
Now, throw a light. (JACK *throws torch through caravan window. Sound of breaking glass.*) You blockhead! Not like that!
JACK. I'm sorry dear. We all can make mistakes.
CAPP (*imitating* JUNE'S *voice*). But soft! What light through yonder window breaks?
CLARICE (*imitating* ROLIO'S *voice*). Oh speak again bright angel, for thou art
 The object of the love of my poor heart.
CAPP. Draw near my sweet, that I may give to thee
   (*Brandishing stick behind his back.*)
Something to warm thy blood most wondrously.
CLARICE (*to* JACK). The hussy! (*Aloud.*) From thy window prithee peek,
  (*Holding her hand out ready to smack.*)
That I may lay my fingers on thy cheek.
CAPP. Come then, my dove.
CLARICE (*approaching*).   I come, my pussy-cat.
CAPP. Take that!
CLARICE.   Take that!
CAPP.   And that!
CLARICE.   And that, and that!
  (*More pandemonium.* JACK *pulls at* CLARICE. MONA *enters* R., *and pulls at* CAPP. ALL *fight and shout.* FAY, LEO *and* SPIKE *enter with lights, and restore order.*)
CLARICE. 'Tis Capp!
CAPP.   'Tis Clarice!
SPIKE (*stepping between them*). That is quite enough.
We're sick and tired of this vendetta stuff.
COMPERE. Why not make friends?
MONA.   Oh yes.
JACK.   Fighting's no fun.
CAPP. Maybe. But where's my daughter?
CLARICE.   Where's my son?
FAY. I'll tell you that. While you were at your strife,
 They entered into partnership for life.
MONA. You mean, they're married?

FAY.   Yes, and better still,
  They've got a double act to top the bill.
         (*Enter* JUNE *and* ROLIO *as a pantomime horse, with* JUNE *in front, naturally. They cavort round, come to a halt in the* C., *and put their heads out.*)
ROLIO. Thus may true lovers evermore abide,
  To hide their difference in a different hide.
JUNE. Sweet ladies, keep your head and you will find
  So long as you're in front, he'll be behind.
COMPERE. Your Graces, my Lords, Ladies and Gentlemen,
  Whether you've paid two bob or one pound ten,
  Whether you telephoned for early booking,
  Or sneaked in when the steward wasn't looking,
  We love you all, and leave you with this thought:
  If everyone behaved just as he ought,
  There'd be no plays, no films and no T.V.—
  Which would be very sad for you and me.
  So, crack the whip! However hard they work us,
  There'll always be a Piccalilli Circus!
         (*Final* CURTAIN, *or a grand procession of all the characters through the audience with big drum beating and loud brass band music.*)

RED HOT CINDERS

A Potted Version of the Cinderella Pantomime in 3 Acts

(But the whole thing lasts only 20 minutes)

by

RICHARD TYDEMAN

This piece of nonsense for a dozen or more characters of either sex is playable on a bare stage or in curtains. Furniture required: one chair. Costumes from the rag-bag. Can be performed with only one rehearsal —or two at the most. Biggest part to learn: eleven and a half lines, except the Compere (who has a book anyway!).

Samuel French – London
New York – Sydney – Toronto – Hollywood

CHARACTERS

The Compère
Cinderella
Her Mother
Lili } *Ugly Sisters*
Grace
Fairy Godmother
Prince Charming
Herald
also Mice, Rats, Courtiers, Guests at the Ball, etc.

(Production Note at end of play)

©1955 by Richard Tydeman

1. This play is fully protected under the Copyright Laws of the British Commonwealth of Nations, the United States of America and all countries of the Berne and Universal Copyright Conventions.

2. All rights, including Stage, Motion Picture, Radio, Television, Public Reading and Translation into Foreign Languages, are strictly reserved.

3. **No part of this publication may lawfully be reproduced in ANY form or by any means—photocopying, typescript, recording (including video-recording), manuscript, electronic, mechanical, or otherwise—or be transmitted or stored in a retrieval system, without prior permission.**

4. Rights of Performance by Amateurs are controlled by SAMUEL FRENCH LTD, 52 FITZROY STREET, LONDON W1P 6JR, and they, or their authorized agents, issue licences to amateurs to give performances of this play on payment of a fee. **It is an infringement of the Copyright to give any performance or public reading of the play before the fee has been paid and the licence issued.**

5. Licences are issued subject to the understanding that it shall be made clear in all advertising matter that the audience will witness an amateur performance; that the names of the authors of the plays shall be included on all announcements and on all programmes; and that the integrity of the author's work will be preserved.

The Royalty Fee indicated below is subject to contract and subject to variation at the sole discretion of Samuel French Ltd.

> Basic fee for each and every
> performance by amateurs   Code B
> in the British Isles

In Theatres or Halls seating Six Hundred or more the fee will be subject to negotiation.

In Territories Overseas the fee quoted above may not apply. A fee will be quoted on application to our local authorized agent, or if there is no such agent, on application to Samuel French Ltd, London.

ISBN 0 573 06615 9

RED HOT CINDERS

ACT 1

The COMPERE *appears before the curtain, carrying a full copy of the script to which he may—and should—refer from time to time.*

COMPERE. Kind friends, we now present before you,
(And we hope we shall not bore you)
A patent, potted Pantomime—
Cinderella, all in rhyme.
I'm the Compere or Commentator,
And as you'll discover later
I'm also prompter, hence my book;
(Excuse me while I take a look)
Ah, yes; now up the curtain goes.

(COMPERE *moves to extreme* L. *of forestage. Curtain up, revealing* CINDERELLA *seated, in rags, weeping before the kitchen fire,* L.)

And right before your very nose
You see poor little Cinderella.
CINDERS. I'm crying 'cos I've got no feller.
COMPERE. Well never mind, look not so glum
Dear Cinderella, here's your Mum.
(Enter MOTHER R.)
CINDERS. She's not my Mum, she's my step-mother;
(We hate the sight of one another.)
COMPERE. The Mother speaks:
MOTHER. Now what's all this?
Get up and help your sisters, miss!
COMPERE. And now here come the ugly sisters—
A pair of most obnoxious blisters.
(Enter Ugly Sisters R. LILY *is thin with a high voice;* GRACE *is fat with a deep voice.)*
What a figure! What a face!
LILY. My name is Lily.
GRACE. Mine is Grace.
LILY. Now Cinders, do me up behind!
GRACE. Come here now Cinders, never mind
About her buttons; do my hair!
(CINDERELLA *runs from one to the bther.)*
COMPERE. So Cinders hurries here and there
Until they're ready to depart,
And Mum and ugly sisters start
To leave for good Prince Charming's Palace;
(Ugly Sisters go off R. MOTHER *gets to the exit.)*
But Cinderella, feeling "jalous"
Says:

CINDERS. Dear step-mother, can't I go?
COMPERE. But step-mamma just answers:
MOTHER. No! (*Exit* MOTHER.)
COMPERE. And now they're gone, poor Cinders cries
And holds her apron to her eyes;
But while she's wiping up her tears
Her Fairy Godmother appears.

(*Enter* FAIRY GODMOTHER, *and stands behind* CINDERELLA.)

CINDERS. I *wish* that I could see the Ball!
COMPERE. The Fairy answers:
FAIRY. So you shall!
COMPERE. Of course she should have said, "You *shawl*",
To rhyme with "I could see the Ball"
It's sometimes hard to make things rhyme,
But then, who cares, in Pantomime?
FAIRY. I am your Fairy God-mamma!
CINDERS. Hurrah.
COMPERE (*prompting*). Hurray.
CINDERS. Hurray!
COMPERE (*approving*). Hurrah.
FAIRY. I wave my magic wand.
COMPERE. Hey presto!
Rags are changed in evening dress to!

(CINDERELLA *throws off outer rags, disclosing Ball-dress.*)

FAIRY. Fetch me a pumpkin, rat and mice.
COMPERE. And Cinders gets them in a trice.
(*Enter* R., *crawling, two* MICE—*small actors, one* RAT—*taller actor, covered with brown or grey blankets.* CINDERELLA *brings on a yellow balloon for a pumpkin.*)
FAIRY. I wave my magic wand once more.
(*Transformation! See Production Note.*)
COMPERE. And up there rises from the floor
A Coach and Horses, all Complete
With Coachman. Cinders takes her seat.
But wait, the Fairy has not done:
FAIRY. The Ball goes on till half past one;
But don't stay after twelve o'clock
Or else your shoes and lovely frock
Will change to rags. Now don't forget!

(*Exit all except* COMPERE, L.—*into fireplace, if any.*)

COMPERE. So off they go! And I will bet
That you all think it rather strange
They drive right through the kitchen range.
But I've seen stranger sights than these!
So ends Act One. The Curtains, please.

(*Curtains close, leaving* COMPERE *outside.*)

ACT II

COMPERE. There is no interval you know,
So we'll continue with the show.
The scene will look the same as ever,
But please imagine, if you're clever,
That we are at Prince Charming's house;
And hark! A dreamy waltz by Strauss.

(*The "Blue Danube" is heard thumped out on a piano, or played on a very tinny gramophone. Curtain rises on several couples dancing.* PRINCE CHARMING *sits,* C. *Dance finishes, and dancers group* L. *and* R.)

See the happy dancers chaffing—
All except the Prince are laughing.
He's alone amidst the whirl:

PRINCE. I'm gloomy 'cos I've got no girl.
COMPERE. Well, cheer up Prince, two beauties come;
(It's Grace and Lily with their Mum.)
(*Enter* R. MOTHER *and Ugly Sisters.*)
MOTHER. Your Royal Highness really oughter
Dance with this, my elder daughter.
(*She pushes* GRACE *forward.* PRINCE *turns away.*)
PRINCE. Tonight no one shall dance with me;
I have a touch of Housemaid's Knee.
COMPERE. That isn't true. But do you blame him?
The ugly sisters, just to shame him,
Dance with each other.
(*Ugly Sisters dance clumsily for a few bars.*)
Oh, my hat.
We've had about enough of that!
(*Enter* CINDERELLA *in Ball-dress,* L.)
But who is this who now appears?
The guests all give three hearty cheers.
Hip hip . . .
GUESTS. Hurrah!
COMPERE. Hip hip . . .
GUESTS. Hurray!
COMPERE. Hip hip . . .
GUESTS. Hurrah!
COMPERE. I cannot say
What makes them happy. Yes I can—
They've seen the Prince—just watch that man,
He's positively truly bitten,
Not to say snookered, sunk, and smitten!
(PRINCE *rises and meets* CINDERELLA.)
PRINCE. Sweet lady, just one dance I crave.
LILY. Cheeky hussy!
GRACE. Saucy knave!
CINDERS. With you, dear Prince, I'd dance till dawn.

LILY.	Well, chase me round the garden lawn!

(PRINCE *and* CINDERELLA *dance for a few bars of soft music.*)

1ST GUEST	I wonder who that girl can be?
GUESTS L.	We do not know.
GUESTS R.	And nor do we.
2ND GUEST.	Perhaps she is a Queen disguised?
LILY.	She's overgrown!
GRACE.	She's undersized!

(*Twelve bangs on a tin tray, off.*)

COMPERE.	The clock is striking twelve. Oh pray,
	Cinderella, run away! (*Exit* CINDERELLA, *running.*)
	But as she leaves, one shoe, size four,
	Falls clattering on the Ballroom floor.
	The Prince runs forward; picks it up;
	He says:
PRINCE.	I will not drink a cup
	Of tea, nor eat my morning kipper,
	Until I find who owns this slipper.
COMPERE.	And now we'll leave this merry throng (*Curtain.*)
	And draw the curtains. Not for long,
	But just to indicate to you
	That's the conclusion of Act Two.

ACT III

COMPERE.	Now, for the last act of our play
	We're back at Cinders' house, next day.

(*Curtain up.* LILY *discovered sitting, holding head;* GRACE *standing, holding stomach.*)

	What's this? The sisters—all alone?
	Can it be hangovers they moan?
LILY.	Oh my poor head!
GRACE.	Oh my poor tum!
LILY.	I wish I hadn't had that rum.
GRACE.	I wish I hadn't had that jelly,
	I've got a pain inside my . . .
COMPERE.	Shelley!
	Byron! Wordsworth! Keats! Defend us,
	No words that rhyme with "jelly" send us!

(*Enter* MOTHER, R.)

	But here comes Mother with some news
	That ought to chase away their blues.
MOTHER.	The Prince's coach on the parade is.
LILY.	Oh, tell the Prince to go to . . .
COMPERE.	Ladies!
MOTHER.	He's come to try the slipper, ducky;
	Why shouldn't one of you be lucky?
COMPERE.	The trumpet sounds. The cannons roar.

(*Appropriate noises from the wings.*)

The Prince is knocking at the door.
HERALD *(off)*. Make way and let Prince Charming pass!
COMPERE. Then enter Prince, with slipper, glass.
  (*Enter* R., HERALD, *carrying slipper on cushion*, PRINCE CHARMING, *and the* COURTIERS—*formerly known as* GUESTS.)
HERALD. All ladies who were at the Dance.
  Can try this slipper.
COMPERE. What a chance
  For these two girls.
GRACE *(sitting)*. Now come on Lily,
  Take my shoe off.
LILY *(pushing* GRACE*)*. Don't be silly,
  You're too old, and you're too fat.
COMPERE. Now ladies, not so much of that.
  Toss up for first. Now you call, Grace.
    (COMPERE *spins an imaginary coin.*)
GRACE. I'll say it's heads.
COMPERE. It is. Now place
  Your foot upon the Herald's cushion,
  And see if the slipper you can push on.
    (GRACE *tries on the slipper.*)
MOTHER. Alas, your heel is much too large.
GRACE. I'll grease it with a lump of marg.
COMPERE. Oh no, you won't. It's plain that you
  Are not the owner of this shoe.
    (LILY *takes* GRACE'S *place on the chair.*)
MOTHER. Let Lily try. Oh dear, your toe
  Into the slipper will not go.
LILY. I'll cut it off and never wince.
COMPERE. No no! I'm very sorry, Prince,
  At least, I mean I'm *glad* to state
  You're saved from an unpleasant fate;
  For neither margarine nor knife
  Will fit these dames to be your wife.
    (*Enter* CINDERELLA, L., *with rags on again.*)
PRINCE. Then let us go and try elsewhere.
  But stay; who is this damsel fair?
MOTHER. Oh, just an orphan working here;
  She was not at your Ball, I fear.
COMPERE. The Prince is not to be denied;
    (CINDERELLA *sits and tries slipper.*)
  He's tried for hours to find his bride.
  And speaking between me and you,
  I think he's getting hungry too,
  For he has vowed he will not eat
  Until he and his lady meet.
HERALD. It fits. (CINDERELLA *throws off rags.*)
LILY. It can't!

GRACE.	Oh, what a cheek!

(PRINCE *and* CINDERELLA *embrace.*)

COMPERE.	The Prince and Cinders cannot speak,
	Except to say to Sis and Mother:
PRINCE AND CINDERELLA.	
	We're happy, 'cos we've got—each other.
COMPERE.	They are too happy even to spy
	That Fairy Godmamma is nigh.

(*Enter* FAIRY GODMOTHER.)

Come Fairy, Father Time is pressing;
Give the happy pair your blessing.

(FAIRY GODMOTHER *stands on chair.*)

FAIRY.	Bless you my children both, and may
	All your troubles fly away.

(*Tableau.*)

COMPERE.	Our play is done. My job is ended;
	Now the least said, the soonest mended.
	Music! Let curtains fall upon
	The Wedding March by Mendelssohn.

(*Piano or gramophone plays "Wedding March". Curtain falls—or better still, all characters march out in procession through the audience.*)

THE END

PRODUCTION NOTE

This is intended to be a complete "rag" and should be played as such —and the "hammier" the better. No attempt should be made at realism, but of course it is important for the players to speak the exact lines allotted to them, no more and no less; otherwise the impact of the atrocious verse will be lost.

Hints on the Transformation Scene: CINDERELLA should wear evening dress, and over it a ragged overall, preferably cut open down the back, so that with a shrug of the shoulders she can slip it off. The two MICE crawl in covered with brown blankets, and the RAT covered with a grey blanket. As the FAIRY waves her wand, CINDERELLA bursts her yellow (pumpkin) balloon with a pin. All stand up, MICE keep blankets on, but hold plumes up to their heads, for they are now horses. RAT throws blanket over left arm, revealing himself as a Coachman, and dons a cocked hat; at the same time he unrolls a large sheet of paper attached to a stick over his right shoulder. On this paper is a crude picture of the side of a coach, with a window cut out of it in the proper place. CINDERELLA stands behind the paper and looks out through the window. On the cue: "Off they go", all exit L., CINDERELLA waving to the audience through the window as they go.

When CINDERELLA runs away at midnight, it is an effective piece of business for her to pause at the side of the stage, and in full view of the audience wrench off her shoe and throw it at the PRINCE'S feet before running off.

FAIRY GODMOTHER can be played either as a "witch" type, or more effectively as an exaggerated pantomime Fairy Queen in ballet dress and spangles.

The COMPERE needs to be a cross between a Circus Ringmaster and a B.B.C. Announcer—with a dash of the Music Hall Chairman thrown in.

WAY OUT WEST!

A Minidrama

by

RICHARD TYDEMAN

A Wild and Woolly Minidrama for about a dozen characters of either sex. As in the same author's *Unhand Me Squire!* the COMPERE has a book, and no one else has more than twelve lines of atrocious verse to learn. No scenery or furniture required; no headaches over costumes or props; few rehearsals needed.

Samuel French – London
New York – Sydney – Toronto – Hollywood

CHARACTERS
in order of their appearance

COMPERE, who has a book
MIRANDY, Judge Sandiman's daughter
JOE, a good man
JAKE, a bad man
MOMMA, Judge Sandiman's wife
JUDGE SANDIMAN himself
THE CURTAIN PULLER
BIG CHIEF, a Red Indian
RUNNING WATER, Big Chief's daughter
SQUARE DANCERS – George, Hank, Caroline, Otis, etc

SCENE : A Ranch, somewhere between Hollywood and Oklahoma.

COPYRIGHT INFORMATION
(See also page ii)

This play is fully protected under the Copyright Laws of the British Commonwealth of Nations, the United States of America and all countries of the Berne and Universal Copyright Conventions.

All rights, including Stage, Motion Picture, Radio, Television, Public Reading, and Translation into Foreign Languages, are strictly reserved.

No part of this publication may lawfully be reproduced in ANY form or by any means — photocopying, typescript, recording (including video-recording), manuscript, electronic, mechanical, or otherwise — or be transmitted or stored in a retrieval system, without prior permission.

Licences are issued subject to the understanding that it shall be made clear in all advertising matter that the audience will witness an amateur performance; that the names of the authors of the plays shall be included on all announcements and on all programmes; and that the integrity of the authors' work will be preserved.

The Royalty Fee is subject to contract and subject to variation at the sole discretion of Samuel French Ltd.

In Theatres or Halls seating Four Hundred or more the fee will be subject to negotiation.

In Territories Overseas the fee quoted in this Acting Edition may not apply. A fee will be quoted on application to our local authorized agent, or if there is no such agent, on application to Samuel French Ltd, London.

VIDEO-RECORDING OF AMATEUR PRODUCTIONS

Please note that the copyright laws governing video-recording are extremely complex and that it should not be assumed that any play may be video-recorded for *whatever purpose* without first obtaining the permission of the appropriate agents. The fact that a play is published by Samuel French Ltd does not indicate that video rights are available or that Samuel French Ltd controls such rights.

PRODUCTION NOTE

The reader will, I hope, have realised that the atrocious verse is written in typical "square dance" rhythm, and the cast should make the most of this so that the whole thing goes "with a swing".

A great deal depends on the COMPERE, who has by far the biggest part; but by way of compensation he is also allowed to have a copy of the script in his hand, and so can act as prompter as well. MIRANDY and JOE are fairly straight parts; JAKE should be as villainous and melodramatic as possible. MOMMA is slow in the uptake, and sees things several seconds after everyone else; the JUDGE makes a lot of noise and takes a drink whenever he can. BIG CHIEF should be as big as possible, RUNNING WATER small and dainty. It does not matter much whether the SQUARE DANCERS can really dance or not. My own favourite part is that of the CURTAIN PULLER, whose brief appearances give an opportunity for real character.

Costumes are easy: coloured shirts and jeans for the men, perhaps with a handkerchief knotted round the neck in cowboy style; long coloured dresses for the ladies, with bonnets. The Red Indians wear dark blankets wrapped round them; RUNNING WATER wears one feather in her hair; a feathered head-dress for BIG CHIEF can be borrowed from any right-minded small boy. Try to get a light-coloured shirt for JOE, and a dark one for JAKE, to emphasise the difference between good and bad.

Anyone who attends the cinema will be able to put on a passable psuedo-American accent, and if they are all different it will be all the funnier.

This Minidrama is obviously written with a mixed cast in mind, but there is no reason why it shouldn't be performed by all women, or all men.

Reckon that's all I need to say.

O.K., Producer, take it away. —R.T.

WAY OUT WEST!

The COMPERE *appears before the curtain, book in hand.*

COMPERE. Hi there, folks! I'm mighty pleased to meet you,
    Sitting there all clean and neat, and in your Sunday best.
But hold on tight now, because we're gonna treat you
    To just a little interlude called "Way Out West!"
(Moving down L. *as curtain rises on empty stage.)*
Up goes the curtain, and what can you see, folks?
    A ranch on the prairie in the still morning air.
Aw shucks, you needn't worry, just do the same as me, folks,
    (You can't see nothing, 'cos there ain't nothing there,)
Use imagination and paint yourself a back-cloth,
    Purple with the mountain-tops and green with the corn;
Weave yourself a tapestry from ordinary sack-cloth,
    And you'll see what you want to see, as sure as you were born.
(Enter, down R. MIRANDY, *a pretty girl. She moves* C.)
First on the scene comes sweet Mirandy Sandiman,
    Pretty as a picture, and whiter than the snow.
(Enter, down R. JOE, *a pleasant young man.)*
    Close on her heels comes faithful Joe the handy-man.

JOE. Oh, Miss Mirandy.
MIRANDY *(without turning).* Why, if it isn't Joe!
COMPERE. That's all put on, folks, *she* knew that Joe was following—
    Watch her eyelids flutter as she turns in mock surprise.
*(*MIRANDY *turns in exaggerated surprise, fluttering eyelids— to* JOE'S *obvious embarrassment.)*
MIRANDY. What *can* you want with me, Joe?
COMPERE.   There, now she's got him wallowing.
JOE. Nothing—well—I mean—
COMPERE.   He's in it—right up to the eyes!
MIRANDY. Yes?
JOE.   Aw, nothing.
MIRANDY.   Nothing, Joe?
COMPERE.   Come on boy, pop the question.
JOE. Miss Mirandy, as you know, I'm not much good at talk—
    It sticks here. *(Indicating his chest.)*
MIRANDY.   What a shame. Perhaps it's indigestion?
JOE. No it's—well I—would you care to take a little walk?

WAY OUT WEST!

COMPERE. Now with her bonnet her eyes Mirandy's shading;
Gently she places her fingers on his arm.
Off they go together. (MIRANDY *and* JOE *go out* L.)
But while they're promenading,
On the scene comes Jake the jackal, meditating harm.
(*Enter down* R. JAKE, *the bad man, with a gun.*)
This here character's a thorough-going bad man—
Never does a stroke of work, and lazes all the day.

JAKE (*looking off* L. *and raising gun*).
Joe, with Mirandy! I'll get him!

COMPERE (*knocking the gun up*). Are you mad, man?
The penalty for murder is to hang—

JAKE (*lowering gun*). O.K., O.K.

COMPERE. Why don't you let them be, Jake?

JAKE. You don't know what you're saying.
I love Mirandy, and she belongs to me.
Anyone who wants her had better start a-praying,
He's surely going to need it. (*Exit up* R.)

COMPERE. There, folks, do you see?
Now don't say a word, 'cos Mirandy's coming back again;
And here comes her Mother on her poor rheumatic legs.
(*Enter down* R. MOMMA, *carrying bucket.*)

MOMMA (*crossly*).
Hens not fed. I shall give that Jake the sack again.
(*Re-enter* MIRANDY L. *carrying her bonnet.*)

MIRANDY. Momma, Joe's proposed to me!

MOMMA (*taking no notice*). We shan't get any eggs.

MIRANDY. Eggs, Momma?

MOMMA. Jake; he's forgot to fill the chicken trough.

MIRANDY. Momma, Joe's proposed to me!

MOMMA (*still grumbling about* JAKE). What *will* that boy do next?

MIRANDY. Momma, will you listen?

MOMMA (*suddenly noticing her*). Why child, you've got your bonnet off.

MIRANDY. I'm going to be married, Momma.

MOMMA (*who still hasn't taken this in*). Where's your self-respect?
Here's five cents; go, buy yourself some candy.

MIRANDY. Momma, you're impossible! (*Exit down* R.)

MOMMA. Yes—*what* was that she said?

COMPERE. She's going to be married, ma'am.

MOMMA. Oh, married—my Mirandy.
(*Suddenly realising what this means.*)
Married?

COMPERE. Sure as eggs is eggs.

MOMMA (*thrusting bucket into his hand*). Here, see them hens is fed;
I got to stop this nonsense. (*Exit down* R.)

COMPERE *(holding up bucket)*. That's what I get for helping.
I'd better go and feed the birds.
(Exit L. Re-enter MOMMA, R.*)*
MOMMA. You didn't tell me who—
Well, never mind, but there's going to be some yelping;
When father loads his shot gun there's no telling what
he'll do!
(Exit down R. Re-enter JAKE *up R.)*
JAKE. I heard all that; and if I'm pretty clever,
Joe is for the high jump, and I'll hang out the flag.
Luck like Joe's just can't go on for ever;
If I play my cards right, Mirandy's in the bag!
(Exit up R. Re-enter COMPERE L. *with basket of eggs.)*
COMPERE. My, my! Folks, them birds deserve their pickings;
Twenty-seven new laid eggs I've taken from the nest.
Twenty-seven eggs, folks, from only twenty chickens—
But that's the way we do things, Way Out West!
(Enter R. JUDGE SANDIMAN. *He has obviously been drinking, and now carries his shot-gun at the ready.)*
JUDGE. I'll shoot him, I'll stab him, I'll twist his cursed throttle!
But first I'll wet my whistle with a drop of gin and
lime.
(Producing an empty bottle.)
Well, of all the rotten luck—another empty bottle!
COMPERE. He's Mirandy's father folks, we'd better play for time.
JUDGE *(throwing away bottle and raising gun again)*.
Where is the man who's after my Mirandy?
Paint a target on his back, and send him down the line.
COMPERE *(producing a brandy flask)*.
Howdy Judge, will you have a spot of brandy?
JUDGE *(putting gun down and taking brandy flask)*.
Them's the nicest words I've heard since eighteen
ninety-nine. *(He drinks.)*
COMPERE. What seems to be the trouble sir?
JUDGE *(centre)*. My wife has just advised me
Some low-down good-for-nothing guy is trying something on.
This information I must admit surprised me—
My wife don't often hear of things till after they've
been done.
(He drinks again. Re-enter quickly, in this order, MIRANDY, JOE, MOMMA, JAKE. *They group themselves on either side of the* JUDGE, *with* MIRANDY *on his left, kneeling to him.)*
MIRANDY. Pop!
JOE (L. *of* MIRANDY). Judge!
MOMMA *(kneeling,* R. *of* JUDGE). Henry!
JAKE (R. *of* MOMMA). Your Honour!
JUDGE. Why now, looky here—

ALL.	Please will you listen to what I have to say?
COMPERE.	What's the betting now folks? I wish I had my bookie here.
JOE.	I—
MOMMA.	You—
MIRANDY.	He—
JAKE.	She—
JUDGE (*trying to speak*).	It—
JOE AND MIRANDY.	We—
MOMMA AND JAKE.	They—

(*Each of them is pointing at one of the others, with the* JUDGE *holding his hands to his ears. In these positions they "freeze" into a tableau. The* COMPERE *walks all round them and shrugs.*)

COMPERE. What a situation! We'll never put it right, folks;
   They'll stay like that for ever if we don't take care.
Call it a day, and put them out of sight, folks;
   Draw the curtain, someone, let's get a breath of air!
(*Curtain falls leaving* COMPERE *outside.*)
Phew, that's better! Ain't you glad we've got a curtain?
(Reckon we could use one in real life, too!)
I ain't sure of much, but one things certain:
   None of these here characters knows what they're gonna do.
Let's have a re-cap, and see where we are now:—
   Jake wants Mirandy, and Mirandy wants Joe;
The Judge wants a drink—he'll be off to find the bar now;
   Momma—well, what Momma wants I really wouldn't know.
Let's move the clock on about three hours.
Open up the curtain and on with the task.

(*Curtain rises. The* JUDGE *is fast asleep, sitting propped up against the back wall or curtain. The others have all gone.*)

Yes, they've all gone, except— By all the powers!
   I quite forgot I'd left a pint of brandy in that flask,
(*Picking up empty flask.*)
Just as I suspected—not a drop left in it,
   And here's the Judge a-sleeping as heavy as a log.
(*Shaking* JUDGE.)
Judge! Hey Judge, will you listen just a minute?
   Wake up, will you!

JUDGE (*sleepily*). . . . and I'll shoot him like a dog.
(*He collapses and lies flat.*)

COMPERE. Gosh, this is terrible! Let's have the curtain down again.
(*Curtain falls behind* COMPERE.)
And really I'm surprised at you; this ain't no time to laugh.

Turn on the clock and push the hands aroun' again;
This time we'll give it an hour and a half.
Curtain up!
CURTAIN-P. *(appearing round edge of curtain).*
Brother, will you make up your mind, please?
COMPERE. Who the heck are you?
CURTAIN-P. Me? I pull the curtain ropes.
COMPERE. You mustn't come out here. Just get back behind, please.
(CURTAIN-P. *disappears.* COMPERE *turns to audience.*)
Don't take any notice; of all the silly dopes!
CURTAIN-P. *(re-appearing).*
I heard you say that, you common commentator.
COMPERE *(threateningly).*
Get back behind there—go on—shoot!
(CURTAIN-P. *disappears.*)
Now on with the show please, ninety minutes later.
Curtain up! *(Curtain rises.)*
That's better. Help! Who are you?
(The JUDGE *has now disappeared. In the centre of the stage stands* BIG CHIEF, *an enormous Red Indian. On a camp stool at his feet sits his daughter* RUNNING WATER.*)*
R. WATER *(in jerky broken English).*
My—name—Gentle—Running—Water,
We—come—here—for—have—Pow—wow.
Him—Big—Chief—and—me—his—daughter.
COMPERE. Pleased to meet you.
R. WATER *(nudging* CHIEF*).* You say—
CHIEF *(very loudly, raising arm).* How!
COMPERE. This is very nice, but we weren't expecting you.
R. WATER. We—come—look—for—pale-face—beau.
COMPERE. Tell me his name, and I'll be directing you.
Will you come this way?
R. WATER *(nudging* CHIEF*).* You say—
CHIEF *(loudly).* No!
COMPERE. Just as you please, but I know most folks;
He'll know me and I'll know him.
Tell me his name and—I don't want to boast folks—
Tell me; his name is—?
R. WATER *(another nudge).* You say—
CHIEF. Jim.
COMPERE. Jim?—who on earth? It's not Jim Trigger,
He's been dead these twenty years.
Can you describe his face and figure?
R. WATER. Handsome—man—with—stick-out—ears.
COMPERE. Stick-out ears and handsome, is he—
Jim?—You're sure you don't mean Joe?

R. WATER.	Yes.	
CHIEF.	No.	
R. WATER.	No?	
CHIEF.	Yes.	
COMPERE.	I'm going dizzy!	

                      Which is it?
R. WATER *(nudge).* You say—
CHIEF.   I don't know.
COMPERE. Lives on the ranch and works for the Judge?
R. WATER.   Yes.
COMPERE. Handsome too—it sounds like Joe.
                  You folks feel you owe him a grudge?
R. WATER.   Yes,
                  He—my—husband.
COMPERE.   What do you know!
                      (To audience.)
                My! This is bad for poor Mirandy.
                Never knew Joe could be such a skunk.
R. WATER. Big—Chief—keep—his—tomahawk—handy,
                  Chop—him—scalp—off;—you say—
CHIEF *(swiping with tomahawk).*   Clunk!
COMPERE *(to audience, after looking cautiously off* L.*).*
                Here they come now. I must get this cat away,
                And her big blood-thirsty pa.
                     (To the others.)
                You want Joe? Well, he went thattaway.
                     (Pointing R.*)*
R. WATER. Thank—you—kindly. You say—
CHIEF.   Ta.

     (RUNNING WATER *picks up her stool, and follows* CHIEF *off*
  R. COMPERE *ushers them off, and stays down* R.*)*

COMPERE. Gosh, what a mess! *(Looking* L.*)* Oh, Joe's not coming;
                I wouldn't care to be in his shoes.
                    (Enter MIRANDY, L.*)*
                Hullo Mirandy. *(To* AUDIENCE.*)* My head's humming.
                    (To MIRANDY.*)*
                Better prepare yourself.
MIRANDY.   Why? What's the news?
COMPERE. Heavy news—too heavy to be carried;
                Joe's already—oh no, I can't go on.
MIRANDY. Joe's already what?—please—*(to* AUDIENCE.*)* You say—
AUDIENCE *(or someone at the back of the hall).* Married!
MIRANDY. Married! Oh! *(She faints into* COMPERE'S *arms.)*
COMPERE *(to* AUDIENCE*).* Now look what you've gone and done!
    (COMPERE *lowers* MIRANDY *to ground, centre, and stands* R.
  Enter JUDGE *with gun* L.*)*
JUDGE.   So! It was *you!* Put your hands in the air sir!

COMPERE (*raising hands*).
  What's that? Hey no, you're making a mistake.
  (JUDGE *stands behind* MIRANDY *and points gun at* COMPERE.
  Enter JAKE, L., *who points his gun at* JUDGE.)
JAKE.   O.K., drop your gun and stand over there, sir.
  (JUDGE *drops gun, raises hands and moves nearer* COMPERE.)
  That's better. (*Enter* JOE, *with gun*, L.)
JOE.   Now put *your* hands up, Jake.
  (JAKE *drops gun, raises hands and moves nearer* JUDGE.
  Re-enter CHIEF *with tomahawk raised. He moves quickly* L.)
CHIEF.   Which—man—Joe?
JOE.   I'm Joe.
CHIEF.   Then—brother,
  Reach—for—sky!
  (JOE *drops gun, raises hands and moves nearer* JAKE. *All four*—COMPERE, JUDGE, JAKE *and* JOE, *are now standing with hands raised. Enter* MOMMA, L. *She points at* MIRANDY.)
MOMMA.   Oh, dear! Oh dear!
  Who dunnit? (CHIEF *points with left hand to* JOE.)
CHIEF.   Him.
JOE (*pointing to* JAKE).   Him.
JAKE (*pointing to* JUDGE).   Him.
JUDGE (*pointing to* COMPERE).   Him.
COMPERE (*looking round and seeing four left hands pointing at him*).
  Mother! Help! Curtain. *Get me out of here!*
  (COMPERE *runs forward as curtain falls behind him*.)
  Gosh, that was close! I nearly gave up hope then.
  Lucky thing they pulled them curtains quick.
CURTAIN-P. (*appearing round curtain*).
  Well, well, well; and who's a silly dope then?
COMPERE.   I'll admit it. (*Shaking his hand*.) You're a brick.
  (CURTAIN-P. *disappears*.)
  Six hours pass; and now for the show-down;
  Bring on the chorus, and give the boys a chance.
  Come with me now to the ranch-house hoe-down.
  Start up the phonograph and let's all dance!
  (COMPERE *moves down* L., *as at first. Curtain up on a* SQUARE DANCE PARTY. *At least two men and two girls are dancing; more if available. Any square dance record*.)
COMPERE (*as the dance ends*).
  Gee, what a party! All the whole parade is here.
  Are you having fun, girls?
GIRLS.   Yes sirree!
COMPERE.   And what about the boys now, with all these lovely ladies here;
  What you got to say, fellers?
MEN.   Yip-iy-ee!
COMPERE.   Now where's Mirandy? I don't see her dancing.

WAY OUT WEST!

1st Girl. Ever since she heard the news she's feeling mighty low.
1st Man. Maybe that Injun girl was sort of just romancing?
2nd Girl. Never would have thought of such a shabby thing of Joe.
2nd Man. Here he is now folks; don't take any notice.
  (Enter Joe. *He comes down* c.*)*
Joe. Hi there! (All *turn away.*) What's the matter? What've I done?
  (Approaching individuals who deliberately ignore him.)
  Hey, George—Hank—Miss Caroline—Miss Otis—
Compere. Reckon they just don't want your company, son.
Joe. Will someone please let me know what the game is?
1st Man. You know well enough without being told.
1st Girl. P'raps he don't remember what the lady's name is.
2nd Man. Does the sound of Running Water turn you Hot and Cold?
  (Enter Judge, *pushing* Mirandy *in front of him. He speaks to* Joe.*)*
Judge. See here! You've got to marry my daughter!
Mirandy. Poppa that's impossible if he's already wed.
Joe. If I'm already *what?* *(Enter* Chief, *dragging* Running Water.*)*
Chief.   Come—Running—Water, Here's—your—husband.
Mirandy.   I wish that I was dead.
Chief *(to* Joe*).*
  You—come—home—to—your—papooses,
  Come—on—quick—now.
R. Water *(pointing to* Joe*).*   That's—not—him!
Chief. What?—you—make—some—more—excuses?
  (Enter Jake, *carrying large box marked "Eggs", followed by* Momma, *down* R.*)*
Momma. Watch your step. Don't drop them.
R. Water *(holding out arms to* Jake*).*   Jim!
Compere. Hold it please! *(Tableau.)* I think I see now. No need to argue any more.
  Jake—or Jim—come here to me now,
  (Joining Jake's *free hand to* Running Waters.*)*
  I pronounce you Man and Squaw.
Joe. Does this mean that I can have Mirandy?
Compere. Sure thing, brother.
Joe.   Honey!
Mirandy *(as they embrace).*   Joe!
Compere. You agree Judge? (Judge *nods.*) That's fine and dandy.
  (To Chief.*)*
  Any objection?
R. Water *(nudge).*   You say—
Chief.   No.

8

WAY OUT WEST!

COMPERE (*coming forward* C., *with* CHIEF, JAKE *and* RUNNING WATER *on his left, and* JOE, MIRANDY, JUDGE *and* MOMMA *on his right, the dancers being grouped behind*).
    O.K. folks, that's the end of the play now;
    Hope we've pleased you, more or less.
   As for the cast (*to* CAST) well, what do you say now,
    Have you enjoyed it?
R. WATER.   We say—
ALL.   Yes!
COMPERE. Now that the final word is spoken,
    Let's have a dance to end the show.
     (*Taking box of eggs from* JAKE.)
   Give me them eggs before they get broken.
     (*Moves across down* L.)
   Honour your partners! Let her go!
   (*Music. All are dancing as the curtain falls.*)

What-Ho Within!

A Minidrama

Richard Tydeman

A SAMUEL FRENCH ACTING EDITION

FOUNDED 1830

SAMUELFRENCH-LONDON.CO.UK
SAMUELFRENCH.COM

CHARACTERS

In the order of appearance

The Minstrel, *who has a book*
Lady Etheldreda, *a Damsel in Distress*
Joe, *the gardener's boy*
Sir Loin, *Baron of Beef*
Baroness Smith, *a Dragon*
A Mechanic
A Gipsy
A Herald
Band and Chorus of Gipsies

SCENE: Outside a medieval castle

This marvellous Minidrama of the Middle Ages requireth little preparation. No character hath e'en a score of lines to learn, while he that playeth the part of the Minstrel (fortunate fellow) hath a book in his hand whence he may prompt the others.

WHAT-HO WITHIN!

The MINSTREL appears before the curtain, dressed in vaguely medieval costume. He can carry a musical instrument if desired, and should also carry a scroll or book of words to which he refers from time to time.

N.B. Just to make the verse even more atrociously medieval, a slight pause or hesitation should be made in the middle of each line.

MINSTREL. Come all ye lords and ladies gay,
And give ye heed to what I say,
As I to you a tale unfold
Of days gone by when knights were bold.
Trala tralee, trala traloo,
(These words won't mean a thing to you,
They're just to give a breathing space,
And let a Minstrel find his place.)
Trala tralee, trala tralow,
(Ah here we are, I've found it now.)
    (Indicating curtain.)
Draw back, draw back this tapestree,
And let's observe what we shall see.
(Curtain rises, revealing a castle wall at back of stage.)
Behold the grim and ancient castle
Of Baron Smith, the King's own vassal.
But Baron Smith is not at home;
He left last year, by way of Rome,
To join the King upon parade,
To take part in the next Crusade.
By now the King and all his crew is
A-building castles out in Suez.
(Trala tralee, trala tralay,
I hope it keepeth fine for they!)
(LADY ETHELDREDA appears on the castle battlements.)
Upon the battlement appears
A damozel of tender years.
She is imprisoned, so 'tis said.
ETHELDREDA. 'tis true I am: imprison-ed.
MINSTREL. O cruel fate that thou shouldst be
Shut up in such adversitee.
ETHELDREDA. I weep.
MINSTREL.   Thou weepest? By my trow,
Then let us weep together now.
    (They both weep loudly.)
(Trala tralee, trala tralunga,
I wish I were but ten years younger!)

1

WHAT-HO WITHIN!

ETHELDREDA. Alas! alas! for whilst thou weepeth,
A Dragon fierce this castle keepeth.
MINSTREL. Oh would that I had horse and waggons,
For I'm allergic unto dragons.
ETHELDREDA. By night and day this Dragon waketh,
And watcheth ev'ry move I maketh.
MINSTREL. O maiden fair, thou seem'st to be
In sorry plight:
ETHELDREDA. Thou tellest me!
MINSTREL. But is there none to take thy part,
And in this reptile plant a dart?
Hast thou no love to give thee joy?
ETHELDREDA. Not one, save Joe, the gardener's boy.
I love him with a passion pure,
Except when he stacks up manure.

(*Enter* JOE, *roughly clad, with a fork over his shoulder. He gazes lovingly at* ETHELDREDA *who returns his gaze.*)

MINSTREL. But here he comes — this ruddy youth.
(Alas the maiden speaks the truth;
Trala tralee, trala traloma,
I do not care for his aroma!)
JOE. That is my Lady Etheldreda;
She is my love since first I seed her.
If from her bondage she were free,
I reckon I could marry she.

(JOE *and* ETHELDREDA *gaze at each other languishingly.*)

MINSTREL. Ah do but see their tender look;
You've read about such things in books.
(I'd like to take my gloves of leather,
And bash their silly heads together!)
Begone young man, I hear the sound
Of someone riding o'er the ground,
His horse a-stumbling on the ruts,—
Or else on shells of cokernuts.

(*Cokernut shells are heard galloping, off.*)

JOE. Fair Etheldreda I'll be gone.
Fear not, I shall return anon.

(JOE *goes out. Galloping ceases.*)

MINSTREL. But what is this? Ah, welcome sight!
I see a doughty valiant knight,
As brave and warlike as a lion,
And clad in sundry bits of iron.

(*Enter* SIR LOIN, *dressed in saucepan lids, coalscuttle, stovepipes, etc., carrying wooden sword and dustbinlid shield.*)

Advancing with a weighty tread,
The knight now lifteth up his head,

WHAT-HO WITHIN!

	Smiteth his shield with horrid din, And loudly calls:
SIR LOIN.	What-ho within!
MINSTREL.	The lady hears his lusty shout, And swift replies:
ETHELDREDA.	What-ho without!
MINSTREL.	On seeing her, the valiant knight, A-dazzled by this wondrous sight, All down on bended knee he falleth.
SIR LOIN.	What-ho, what-ho!
MINSTREL.	Again he calleth. The maiden cries in agonee,
ETHELDREDA.	Oh hast thou come to rescue me?
SIR LOIN.	That was the aim I had in view. I'd like to see much more of you.
MINSTREL.	But though his eye he is a-winking, He doesn't mean what you are thinking. (Trala tralee, trala tralonce, And "Honi soit qui mal y pense!") Then from his knee he riseth so. (SIR LOIN *tries unsuccessfully to rise*.) I said he riseth.
SIR LOIN.	Yes, I know; I think I'm stuck — can't move my shanks.
MINSTREL.	I'll help you up. That's better.
SIR LOIN (*rising with help*).	Thanks. This armour puts me in a panic; My squire is not a good mechanic.
MINSTREL.	Thou sayest truth, thy joints are rusty, Thy sump is dry, thy windscreen dusty, Thy springs, thy brakes, and thy suspension Require immediate attention. So may we draw the curtain please, To give him time to oil his knees. (*Curtain falls leaving* MINSTREL *outside*.) And now for just a little while, I will for you the time beguile By telling of the latest joke;— 'twill make you laugh until you choke. The other day a knight I spied, A beauteous damsel by his side; When next we met I ask him, "Prithy, Who was that damsel I saw with thee?" With sparkling wit this answer made he, "No damsel she — that was my Lady!" (Trala tralee, trala traluma, What wondrous medieval humour!)

WHAT-HO WITHIN!

But let's return to our poor knight,
And see if all has been put right.
(Curtain rises. A MECHANIC has just finished work.)

MECHANIC. 'tis done, my Lord, thou'rt oiled and greased.
Our charges have of course increased.
This job will cost you thirty shillin'.
SIR LOIN. Just tell your boss to send the bill in.
MECHANIC. Good day, sir knight. Don't go too fast.
Until five hundred miles are past,
Thou shouldst not raise thy motive power
To more than thirty miles on hour.
(MECHANIC goes out.)
MINSTREL. Come then, good sir, this doleful maid
Most earnestly requireth aid.
Wilt thou the Dragon take or kill?
SIR LOIN. Upon this sword I swear I will.
MINSTREL. Now thou hast sworn, make no mistake,
To kill or else somehow to take
A fearsome creature, oh rash boy,
Of this thy task I wish thee joy.
(Trala traloo, trala tralee,
I'd rather it was him than me!)
But soft! What doth yon maiden say?
She pointeth now the other way.
ETHELDREDA. Oh fly, sir knight, the Dragon cometh!
MINSTREL. This news my limbs and vitals numbeth.
There is no time to fly, I fear.
Let's just pretend we are not here.
(MINSTREL flattens himself against proscenium arch. SIR LOIN kneels in a heap, with his face to the ground. Enter BARONESS SMITH, an imposing lady, made up to look elderly, but with bright, carrot-coloured hair escaping from her head-dress.)
ETHELDREDA. I saw you coming, Step-mamma;
I'm very pleased to see you.
BARONESS.   Pah!
You'd better mind your manners, Miss;
And tell me pray just what is this?
(She points at SIR LOIN. MINSTREL bows.)
MINSTREL. O marv'lous fair and beauteous Madam,
(BARONESS looks pleased at this.)
Although I know him not from Adam,
Beneath this heap of metal scrap
There lies a very decent chap.
BARONESS. Get up, get up, thou fallen fellow.
SIR LOIN *(without looking up).*
Methought me heard the Dragon bellow.

WHAT-HO WITHIN!

BARONESS. What's that you say?
SIR LOIN.   Some creature slimy
Is calling me. Where is it? *(Looking up.)* Blimey!
BARONESS. O noble youth look not so haughty;
'tis true that I'm — er — approaching forty.
But still I have a heart that can
Appreciate a handsome man.
(She raises him and smiles at him lovingly.)
MINSTREL. Now this is all most complicated.
The Dragon is infatuated;
And now his name she doth demand.
SIR LOIN. Sir Loin of Beef, at thy command.
MINSTREL. She tells him hers, it is no less
Than Sarah Smith, the Baroness.
And then she adds with playful purr,
BARONESS. My friends all call me "Carrots" sir.
MINSTREL. I find this conduct pretty rotten,
Poor Etheldreda is forgotten;
As on they chat, this pair of parrots,
The bold Sir Loin of Beef, and Carrots,
(Trala tralee, trala tralenu,
I'm glad that I'm not on their menu!)
Upon the walls the damsel fair
Now waves her arms in wild despair,
And calleth to Sir Loin so brave,
ETHELDREDA. Hey there, its *me* you came to save!
(She waves wildly and kisses her hand to SIR LOIN *who takes no notice. Re-enter* JOE.)
MINSTREL But this display hath filled with pain
The heart of Joe, her faithful swain.
JOE. Alas, alack! The little goose;
She tries to play both fast and loose.
MINSTREL. I sympathise, and yet, you know,
I do not understand you, Joe.
I've never met in days gone past,
A girl who was both loose and fast.
(Trala tralee, trala tralad,
Ah me, I only wish I had!)
But now to change this doleful mood,
There comes a pleasant interlude.
(Enter GIPSIES, *any number from two upwards.)*
A Gipsy Tribe with ribbons flying;
Pray wither, tell me, are you hieing?
GIPSY. O Minstrel we are on our way
To Epsom Downs for Derby Day.
But if it won't from work detain you,
We'll stay awhile and entertain you.

MINSTREL *(to audience).*
        It's always nice, you will agree,
        To have a good varietee;
        So as a change from all this piffle,
        The Gipsy Band will play some skiffle.
    (The GIPSIES *can either play music here, with song and dance if required, or else they can pretend to play while a gramophone record is put on. At the end, the other characters applaud.)*
        O Gipsies, thanks, that's quite enough.
        (To audience.)
        I never heard such frightful stuff.
        Let those applaud who wish to do so;
        If that was music, I'm Caruso!
        The gipsies now take round the hat;
        They won't get very rich on that.
        (Trala tralee, trala tralunion,
        We don't do this in the Minstrels' Union.)

GIPSY.   Good day, kind friends. For we must go.
        We hope you've all enjoyed our show.
        May happiness and health be in you;
        And now our journey we'll continue.
        (GIPSY BAND *goes out.*)

MINSTREL.   Now you are wond'ring, are you not,
        How Gipsies come into our plot?
        Of course they don't. We tried to lose them,
        But as we failed we had to use them.
        And now we must lost time amend,
        And bring our story to an end.
        I fear Sir Loin of Beef has come
        Beneath the Baroness's thumb.
        (SIR LOIN *kneels before* BARONESS.)
        He asketh her to be his bride;—
        He knoweth not her hair is dyed.
        (For dyeing hair the latest rage is
        Of the middle-aged in the Middle Ages.)
        On seeing this the gardener Joe
        Takes vengeance on his ancient foe,
        And cries,

JOE.   Sir Knight, though she's inhuman,
        This lady is a married wooman!
        (SIR LOIN *jumps up.*)

MINSTREL   At this the knight springs back in terror;
        He sees he's made a ghastly error.
        For by his oath he must, and will
        As bride her take or else her kill!
        He lifts his sword of monstrous size,
        While Etheldreda hides her eyes.

WHAT-HO WITHIN!

     Nay, hold Sir Knight. Oh stay thy hand;
     A Herald comes from foreign land.
      (Enter a HERALD.*)*
     Good Herald swift, thy news confess.
HERALD.   Which one of you's the Baroness?
BARONESS. 'tis I.
HERALD.   Then pray for news prepare;
     Thou art, I fear, a Dowagare.
BARONESS. I am a what?
HERALD.   I should have said
     That Baron Smith, deceased, is dead.
     On point of sword with horrid jerks
     He died a-fighting of the Turks.
    (Hands BARONESS *a telegram and goes out.)*
BARONESS. The Baron dead? Then I'am free,
     Sir Loin, my dear, to marry thee.
     (She crushes SIR LOIN *to her bosom.)*
MINSTREL. Oh let these words and let these looks
     Be printed in School History Books.
     This moment shall be known forthwith
     As The Relief of Lady Smith!
  (Exeunt SIR LOIN *and* BARONESS. *Galloping heard, off.)*
     The Dragon's gone. The danger's past.
     Come down sweet maid, you're free at last.
ETHELREDA. Alas, I can't, for yesterday
     She came and took the stairs away.
MINSTREL. Oh this is worse than e'er I knew.
     Quick, tell me Joe, what can we do?
JOE.   Well, if thou lookest round the back,
     Thou'lt see I've made a lovely stack.
     If Ethel jumps, with any luck
     She'll land right on my heap of manure.
 *(*ETHELDREDA *jumps down at the back, and joins* JOE *on stage.)*
MINSTREL. The lady jumps and safely landing,
     By Joseph's side she's now a standing.
     His homely scent she smells no longer,
     For hers if anything is stronger.
     (Exeunt ETHELDREDA *and* JOE.*)*
     Our tale is done, our maiden free,
     Our Dragon foiled. 'Tis time for tea.
     But ere we go I feel quite sure
     You'd like to see them all once more.
     (Galloping heard off. Re-enter ALL.*)*
     Assemble please, your bow to take,
     'ere to the bar our way we make.
  *(*ALL *take a bow. Then* MINSTREL *steps forward.)*
     If you are seeking for a moral,
     With this advice you will not quarrel:—

WHAT-HO WITHIN!

	Keep clear, I'd say as your adviser,
	From Dragons and from Fertiliser.
	Be not with Knights and Gipsies trafficking,
	Who can't tell Ladysmith from Mafeking.
	Remember who to you these hints tells,
	And evermore be kind to Minstrels.
ALL	Trala tralee, trala tralay,
	We'll see you all another day.

CURTAIN

PRODUCTION NOTE

The setting for *What-ho Within!* is very simple. Only one piece of scenery is required, representing a castle wall. If you do not possess such a piece, you can make do with a curtain or a folding screen, with a table behind it for ETHELDREDA to stand on. To make it quite clear what this is supposed to be, various notices could be pinned on the screen, such as: "Baron Smith's Castle. Established 1066," etc. It might also add to the fun to have a direction sign: "Visitors this way. 2/6 each."

Suitable costumes can be found in most property-boxes and rag-bags. The MINSTREL should, if possible, wear tights, a coloured coat or doublet, and a floppy hat with a feather in it. The ladies wear long dresses, and tall conical hats with a wisp of veiling attached to the top. SIR LOIN'S armour can consist of all the ironmongery he can find. JOE requires only a sack with holes cut in it for his head and arms, a piece of string round his waist, and bare legs. GIPSY costume seems to have been more or less the same throughout history, so this should be easy. The MECHANIC and the HERALD can either be genuinely medieval, or if preferred they could be modern — the MECHANIC in overalls and the HERALD in postman's uniform!

Play at a good pace, stick to the script and exaggerate the rhythm. The little hesitation in the middle of each line should not be allowed to disappear. The MINSTREL'S part should be recited in a doleful sing-song sort of voice — indeed he can sing the whole thing if you like, in a mournful minor medieval key. The "trala tralee" bits are certainly more effective if they can be sung. The last couplet of the play can be altered to suit your audience, or the time of year; e.g.—"Trala tralee, trala traligh, Long Live the Newport W.I." or "Trala tralee, trala tralistmas, We wish you all a Merrie Christmas," etc.

There is no reason why *What-ho Within!* should not be performed entirely by women, or entirely by men, if a mixed cast is not available.   —R.T.

www.ingramcontent.com/pod-product-compliance
Ingram Content Group UK Ltd.
Pitfield, Milton Keynes, MK11 3LW, UK
UKHW021841140426
5217IPUK00022B/1543